wicazō ša review

A Journal of Native American Studies

Guest Editor
Nancy Marie Mithlo, University of Wisconsin, Madison

Editor
James Riding In, Arizona State University

Associate Editor
Amy Lonetree, University of California, Santa Cruz

Founding Editors
Elizabeth Cook-Lynn
Roger Buffalohead
Beatrice Medicine
William Willard

Contributing Editors
Duane Champagne, University of California, Los Angeles
Steven J. Crum, University of California, Davis
Ellen Cushman, Michigan State University
Clayton Dumont, San Francisco State University
Donald Fixico, Arizona State University
Julia Good Fox, Haskell Indian Nations University
Lawrence Gross, University of Redlands
Joy Harjo, University of California, Los Angeles
Suzan Shown Harjo, The Morning Star Institute
Tom Holm, University of Arizona
Craig Howe, Oglala Lakota College
Ted Jojola, University of New Mexico
Glenabah Martinez, University of New Mexico
Cornel Pewewardy, Portland State University
Lisa Poupart, University of Wisconsin, Green Bay
Kathryn Shanley, University of Montana
Luci Tapahonso, University of Arizona
Laura Tohe, Arizona State University
Edward Valandra, University of South Dakota, Vermillion
Michael Yellow Bird, Humboldt State University

WICAZO SA REVIEW · SPRING 2012 · VOL 27 NO 1

Special Issue: American Indian Curatorial Practice

CONTENTS

Guest Editor's Introduction
Curatorial Practice and Native North American Art

Nancy Marie Mithlo

What is American Indian Curatorial Practice and why is it important now? Since the 2004 opening of the Smithsonian National Museum of the American Indian on the national mall in Washington, D.C., it may appear that issues of accurate and sensitive self-representations had largely been resolved. Native peoples were no longer routinely being showcased in diorama settings alongside stuffed elephants, as they were in the natural history museum setting. But American Indian scholars and activists discovered that we are now only beginning the process of reclamation of self via the museum enterprise. The enduring tensions surrounding American Indian history, arts, and culture are still with us: traditional or modern, tribally specific or pan-tribal, members of U.S. society or separatist nations.

Self-definition in the institutionalized era of Native representations requires an engagement with existing systems of reception and circulation, including the language, institutions, and concepts that were mobilized in the past to oppress. The museum as a context is simply a building, the exterior manifestation of prevalent ways of thinking and acting. While we can create newer models of exhibition, programming, and even architecture, the real infrastructure lies in the thoughts and actions of the senders and receivers—the theorists and the public who consume messages. As contributing author and curator Michelle McGeough reminds us, this is an act of storytelling, an enduring process at which Indigenous people are known to excel. Her contribution to this volume exposes the complexities of Native participation in the museum enterprise, including the tensions inherent in pan-tribal consultations. In her words, "As a person from the northern prairie who was not privy to the Southwest's indigenous peoples protocol, I was cautious. For me, there is also concern that communities vary in terms of the degree of disclosure that is permissible regarding their spiritual practices. And to an indigenous person there is also the recognition that even in those seemingly benign depictions of everyday life are elements of ceremony and sacredness."

Similarly, artist and curator Miles Miller charts his professional course serving as a curator while negotiating the complexities of relying on inaccurate historical documents that inform the Native American Graves Protection and Repatriation Act regulations. His negotiations appear to involve less a tension between tribes and more a matter of intertribal recognition and acceptance of his traditional training as a Yakama person. He states, "Traditional culture thrives today due to the nurturance of stories that are carried by individuals responsible for their continuance. These community experts serve as curators not only in an object-centered sense, but also in a broader philosophical sense within their tribal contexts. They thus curate not only objects, but also deep spiritual knowledge. This spiritual knowledge highlights notions of ownership and use." These applied, yet deeply theoretical insights by Native arts practitioners, are vital to our understanding of emergent themes and directions in curatorial processes.

Now that we are telling the rich stories of our lives, what stories do we choose and how do we go about the telling? Will established languages—those belonging to the disciplines of art history or curatorial studies—be of use, or are new terms and concepts needed? The researcher John Paul Rangel suggests linkages with TribalCrit theory, citing Walter Benjamin to argue that reduction and simulation in Native arts silence and erase the originating cultures. He suggests adopting the conceptual framework "contemporary" in a strategic manner, in order to assert a Native presence utilizing Indigenous perspectives and aesthetics defined by the case study example of the Museum of Contemporary Native Arts (MoCNA) in Santa Fe, New Mexico. Rangel's contribution highlights the "Indigenization of space" that occurs when Native people "reclaim a location through cultural signifiers, performance, ceremony, song, dance, or installation that convey the existence and presence of Native peoples and cultures." Importantly, MoCNA accomplishes this Indigenization of space by the staff's role as "ambassadors for Native America." His poetic description cites MoCNA as "a contemporary Native arts museum . . . in a U.S. government building that is near the center of a town that was built over a Pueblo Indian village. Over a few hundred years, Native Americans have symbolically reclaimed a small island of the lands they once occupied freely."

The contributing author and artist Dyani Reynolds-White Hawk similarly mines the existing literature to find new paths for emerging theory. Her contribution takes on intersecting parallels with outsider arts and Native arts, locating applications of "otherness," exoticism, and biography that uniquely inform a critical reception in commerce and the academy. She insightfully pinpoints "the ways in which mainstream art institutions and their constituents tend to treat groups that have not historically been equal participants in the makeup of Western art history," concluding that they are "fleeting interests": "Each are brought into mainstream institutions in a manner similar to what we would expect of an invited guest, at times even an honored guest. While we may exalt and care for a guest, when the visit is over, we expect them to leave, at which point our lives return to the comfort of what we know."

A key theme to emerge from these essays is the Indigenous values of mentorship and honoring those who have served in leadership positions. The Museum of Contemporary Native Arts curator Patsy Phillips's original essay on her friend and mentor, the artist Harry Fonseca, extends the work he pursued in series like the *Coyote* by explicitly linking a harsh political history to the restricted circulation and reception of contemporary Native arts today. "Land appropriation, substandard housing and education, limited economic opportunities, and cultural bias are consistent factors in Indian communities," writes Phillips. "These obstacles have negatively affected the self-perception of Indian peoples for generations. This oppressive climate is apparent in the selective venues in which Native arts circulate—galleries, museums, and seasonal arts fairs with restricted categories of reception. Through Coyote, Fonseca suggests, 'Freedom is the Native Americans' choice.'"

Our arts are significant because they offer a platform to creatively express the rage, passion, and strength of our human condition. The physicality of arts offers a tangible way into our psyche and a way out for our survival and prosperity. Given the often brutal and restrictive manifestations of Native peoples as solely living in the past or as inauthentic shadows of their ancestors, the act of creating, reproducing, and circulating one's own stories becomes a form of cultural survival. The United Nations Declaration on the Rights of Indigenous Peoples Article 11 identifies the visual and performing arts as important manifestations of Native peoples' "right to maintain, protect and develop the past, present and future manifestations of their cultures."[1]

Research conducted over the past two generations has resulted in an emerging practice where our students are now instructing other students in a field that is largely unrecognized—the curation of Native arts using Indigenous epistemologies. The signifiers of this field—work that is long-term, reciprocal, mutually meaningful, and with mentorship—are evident in the careful practices that characterize an in-depth analysis, not merely a physical description of an object or a personal, subjective reflection of meaning. heather ahtone's essay in this volume epitomizes this approach, which she terms "Indigenous epistemologies." Her essay explains, "While every effort of political and religious assault has been made historically to subdue these same cultures, their survival can be partially attributed to the continued production of the visual and per-formance arts. As long as Indigenous people continue to use the arts to reflect unique experiences within a contemporary society, they are fundamentally breathing life into these cultures. Because the vitality of these cultures is so closely tied to the creative process, it is important that work by Indigenous artists be considered within a framework that incorporates Indigenous epistemology."

Like Phillips, ahtone credits the arts with the transformative power of continued existence in cultural contexts that are both physical and mental. Artists create spaces of survival, as in Joe Feddersen's 2003 *Urban Indian* glass series, which incorporates the traditional symbols found in his tribe's Plateau-based cultural materials.[2] Working directly with the artist, ahtone incorporates into her analysis specific commu-nity referents for signs and symbols, such as the chevron (an indicator for woman). She concludes, "The idiosyncratic nature of Indigenous designs and symbols puts a responsibility on the artist and art historian to consider these as semiotic references in context with their mean-ings," describing this type of analysis as a form of "reciprocity."

These field-defining referents—context, reciprocity, cultural specificity—are reflected vividly when we conduct critiques of exist-ing scholarly resources. While significant work has been done in the past two generations, the utility of standard paradigms of interpreta-tion, such as regional or chronological referents alone, are now being questioned. Melanie Herzog and Sarah Stolte's essay chronicling the scholarship of recent publications is essential to gaining a perspective of the many theoretical approaches at play. Their careful and insightful analysis charts strategies and resources for teaching American Indian art survey courses as an intellectual exercise, advocating "a reconcep-tualization of art history's discursive frameworks, canonical narratives, and assumptions about art, artists, and representation." Thus, Herzog and Stolte argue, "critical engagement with indigenous methods and knowledge is crucial to this reframing, and must be foregrounded as key course content." Their essay productively expands the analysis from one of Native or non-Native practitioners to a consideration of Native methodologies and perspectives incorporated into the core teaching approaches. "Whether Native or non-Native," they write, "as educators we all need to center Native perspectives in our teaching as we design and instruct courses that look at the interconnections in Native art among aesthetics, materials, function, meaning, social relations, and social practices, and the historical circumstances within which these works of art are produced."

In a parallel fashion, my own essay in this volume formalizes a critique that I typically find employed in conversations on Native arts—the refrains "I'm an artist first and an Indian second," and "There's no word for art in my language." These complaints that originate from within our communities tend to be deeply divisive and unproductive in terms of intellectual discourse and political transformation. My analysis of "post-Indian" curatorial themes seeks to highlight the utility of American Indian Curatorial Practice as a means of reclaiming cultural traditions, asserting sovereignty, and embracing land-based philosophies.

All art is deeply embedded in cultural references and meanings, and not merely apolitical or decorative. While an exposure of the limitations of classic art historical approaches may yield useful insights, I advocate the identification of unique pedagogical practices already at play in institutions and classrooms that actively seek to employ Indigenous perspectives, methodologies, and insights into their interpretation and analysis of contemporary Native arts. Current symposiums and conferences, such as the 2009 School for Advanced Research seminar "Essential Aesthetics: An Exploration of Contemporary Indigenous Art and Identity" and the resulting 2011 conference "Essentially Indigenous? Contemporary Native Arts Symposium," held at the George Gustav Heye Center National Museum of the American Indian, indicate new directions for theorization.

This maturation of the field would be impossible without the institutions that have typically been cast in the role of the cultural inhibitors—museums, research centers, granting agencies, and colleges. Researchers would do well to closely examine the emergence and intersection of these institutions and their long-range impact on American Indian studies more broadly. For example, the Ford Foundation, led by the Cherokee researcher Elizabeth Theobald Richards (program officer for media, arts, and culture), funded nine innovative arts projects across Native North America under the rubric *Advancing the Dialogue on Native American Arts in Society (ATD)* in the first decade of the twenty-first century. I was fortunate to lead one of those projects at the University of Wisconsin, Madison, which I titled "American Indian Curatorial Practice: State of the Field."[3] This issue of *Wicazo Sa Review* is one of the projects that emerged from that initiative.[4]

The final Ford Foundation report released in 2008 identified the long-term aim of the *ATD* initiative to "advance an exchange of ideas by and about the Native American arts field and to engage the larger field in a dialogue around the pluralistic role of arts in society." Critical goals included increasing critical writing by and about the Native American arts community; increasing artistic and scholarly exchanges between Native artists and organizations and other communities in the larger arts field; and expanding participation of Native American arts leaders in key conversations and initiatives on the changing role of arts in the United States. Importantly, the Ford initiative identified the central challenge in achieving these goals as "the current lack of representation and mere inclusion of Native American artists in contemporary art museums, galleries, theaters, dance, and musical venues as well as among regional funders, and diversity commissions." The cumulative finding was that "the cost of accommodating/assimilating their [Native artists'] work to fit the dominant worldview of what counts as 'art' is at best limiting and at worst exploitive. Therefore, this initiative is not about the inclusion of another ethnic group into the broader arts and cultural landscape. It is, rather, about carving a space where contemporary and traditional Native American artists and arts scholars can be a creative and intellectual force for the nation as a whole to examine and further understand its cultural meaning."[5]

This volume offers evidence of the impulse to redefine the parameters of Native intellectual traditions in arts criticism and practice. Scholars have only recently pursued the articulation, codification, and legitimization of American Indian arts drawing from Indigenous epistemologies. Formal and descriptive considerations alone are no longer acceptable in the wake of the intellectual and legal mandates of the past two decades (including the Indian Arts and Crafts Act of 1990 and the Native American Graves Protection and Repatriation Act) dealing with the contextual and political ramifications of American Indian arts production, circulation, and interpretation. Resources and infrastructure such as reference collections, instructional image banks, and textbooks are markedly missing from the study of contemporary American Indian arts. The emerging scholarship profiled in this volume is thus positioned within a transitional period that is establishing new pedagogies, practices, and interpretative frameworks. The formal manifestation of our stories and achievements will prove critical in the incorporation of Indigenous knowledge in arts scholarship.

The curator Lowry Stokes Sims has incisively described the power inherent in "self-definition and self-image" as a revolution for black artists "as they assumed the role of proactive rather than reactive agents in contemporary society."[6] This shift in perception, meaning and action has decisively taken place in Indian country. We need only to recognize, celebrate, and codify the shift for the next generation of intellectuals and activists. This volume does exactly that. My heartfelt

Leatrice Jay *(seated, in glasses, holding girl)* at Mithlo family feast, 2010, Apache, Oklahoma. Photograph by Nancy Marie Mithlo.

thanks go out to the generosity of the authors, artists, and institutions that have made this collection of essays possible.

POSTSCRIPT

I dedicate this volume to my aunt Leatrice Pewewardy Jay, who passed away during the final edits of the manuscript. "Miss Jay" was a gifted, lifelong educator who tirelessly gave herself to the needs of others. Her spirit infuses the work described within these pages. Her strength and passion will not be forgotten.

Nancy Marie Mithlo is a Chiricahua Apache, a PhD, and associate professor of art history and American Indian studies at the University of Wisconsin, Madison. She is the author of *"Our Indian Princess": Subverting the Stereotype* (2009). Mithlo's extensive relationship with the Institute of American Indian Arts includes serving as senior editor for the Ford Foundation–funded volume *Manifestations: New Native Art Criticism*, produced and published by the Museum of Contemporary Native Arts. She received the 2011–2012 School for Advanced Research Anne Ray Fellowship and a Georgia O'Keeffe Research Center Fellowship in support of her publication and exhibit on the legacy of Kiowa photographer Horace Poolaw. Mithlo's curatorial work has resulted in six exhibits at the Venice Biennale.

1 See http://www.un.org/esa/socdev/unpfii/en/declaration.html.

2 Feddersen is from the Okanagan people, who are part of the Colville Confederated Tribes.

3 See the Ford Foundation's 2010 "Native Arts and Cultures: Research, Growth, and Opportunities for Philanthropic Support" report, http://www.fordfoundation.org/pdfs/library/Native-Arts-and-Cultures.pdf. The original portfolio "Advancing the Dialogue on Native American Arts in Society" included the following recipients: Cornell University, the Denver Art Museum, the Institute of American Indian Arts, New York University's Hemispheric Institute of Performance and Politics, the New York Shakespeare Festival's Public Theater, the Smithsonian Institution's National Museum of the American Indian, the University of California, Davis, the University of California, Los Angeles, and the University of Wisconsin–Madison.

4 For other outcomes, see http://www.nancymariemithlo.com/aicp_menu.htm.

5 The Ford Foundation's unpublished "Indigenous Knowledge and Expressive Culture Portfolio Final Report: Advancing the Dialogue on Native American Arts in Society Initiative Convening Held at the Ford Foundation on April 29, 2008"; Elizabeth Theobald Richards, Program Officer, Media, Arts, and Culture, Ford Foundation; JoAnn K. Chase, Consultant, The Chase Group; Sandy Grande, Research Consultant, Ford Foundation.

6 Lowery Stokes Sims, "The Postmodern Modernism of Wilfred Lam," in *Cosmopolitan Modernisms*, ed. Kobena Mercer (Cambridge: MIT Press, 2005), 87.

Indigenous Curatorial Practices and Methodologies

Michelle McGeough

What does indigenous curatorial methodologies mean in terms of curation, and how does an indigenous model of curation differ from that of a Western model? Forward thinkers such as the art historian Nancy Marie Mithlo and the curator Ryan Rice describe indigenous curatorial exhibition projects as utilizing a process of consultation and mentorship, as opposed to a Western notion in which individuality and authorship are highly valued.[1] Although this individualism is most apparent in early ethnographical displays of Native Americans, it is still evident in contemporary Western practice in which the curator maintains a position of authority and is seen as the interpreter for the masses.

The purpose of my discussion is not to critique the Western model of curation, but rather to present two examples of how indigenous methodologies and practices that Mithlo and Ryan cite are presently taught and utilized in the curatorial field. The first example emphasizes the notion of mentorship and demonstrates how this practice is integrated into the curriculum presently being taught in the museum studies program at the Institute of American Indian Art (IAIA), in Santa Fe, New Mexico. The second example is an examination of my experience as the curator of the exhibition *Through Their Eyes: Indian Painting in Santa Fe, 1918–1945* at the Wheelwright Museum of the American Indian (May 17, 2009–April 18, 2010). My focus in this instance is on how the process of consultation was used throughout various stages of this project, and more important, how it was used to bring together what may have been competing interests.

The museum studies program at the Institute of American Indian Arts is one of the oldest in the United States.[2] The IAIA was created by an act of Congress in 1962; a federally funded institution, it offers an associate of fine arts and bachelor of arts degrees in all its disciplines, in addition to a masters of arts in creative writing. In 1972, IAIA created a museum studies program to meet the needs of tribal communities. Originally, the department offered a certificate and an AFA degree. The focus of the program was to teach Native Americans museum practices so that students could return to their communities to assist or become administrators of tribal cultural centers or museums.[3] At that time, the museum and the Institute were located on the grounds of the Santa Fe Indian Boarding School. In 1977, the institute moved to the College of Santa Fe campus, but the museum remained on the boarding school's grounds until 1992, when the Institute of American Indian Arts acquired a federal building in downtown Santa Fe that would become what is now the Museum of Contemporary Native Arts (MoCNA). Museum studies classes were taught at this downtown location as well as on campus. In the 1990s, the museum was primarily a teaching institution, as demonstrated by the fact that under the direction of Chuck Dailey, chair of the museum studies department, the students enrolled in the museum problems class designed and installed many of the new museum exhibitions at MoCNA.

By the fall of 1999, the courses being offering by the department had increased to seventeen. Since the late 1990s, the department has incorporated indigenous worldviews into its curriculum, a move that has become an even greater priority for museum studies in the last five years. In 2005, a new facility for museum studies was added to the hundred-acre campus of the IAIA in southern Santa Fe. The building consists of studios, classrooms, and a teaching art gallery called the Primitive Edge. This gallery space is an integral part of the museum studies curriculum, especially for Exhibitions I and II classes. Exhibition I is primarily a hands-on course in exhibition preparation. Students learn mount making, framing, matting, and generally serve as a volunteer work crew for the four student exhibitions presented each semester in the gallery space.

The Exhibitions II curriculum was built on the foundations of Exhibitions I but was dropped in 2005 and replaced by Museum Studies 240: Telling Our Stories: Museum Curatorial Practices and Methodologies. The intent of this course is for students to understand the process of planning an exhibition, including preparing and presenting an exhibition proposal. Based on a consensus among the students in the class, one proposal is chosen for the winter exhibition. This provides the students with a shared experience of being responsible for one of the exhibitions presented in the Primitive Edge Gallery, where deadlines are real and consequences immediate. Students are responsible for putting out a call for artwork, processing submissions, preparing the artwork for installation, completing the installation, preparing print publicity, catering, and documenting the artwork and exhibition. Although the planning stages may take eight to ten weeks, the actual installation of the exhibition is two weeks, and scheduled class time is only five hours per week. The role of the instructor as a mentor to the students is to make suggestions and point out potential problems; however, it is ultimately the students' exhibition.

Although the students have only months to put together their exhibition, it is a normally a process that can take years. Such was the case of the Wheelwright Museum of the American Indian's exhibition *Through Their Eyes: Indian Painting in Santa Fe, 1918–1945*. I was hired as the curator of this exhibition, with little knowledge of the beginnings of easel painting in the United States or the protocol of the Southwest indigenous people. Whether it was through divine guidance or sheer desperation, I found it imperative to employ a consultative process throughout various stages of the exhibition.

Native American stakeholders have consistently advocated for specific changes in the ways that Native American people and their stories are to be presented in institutions such as museums. In both the United States and Canada, protests by Native American people regarding the display and interpretation of our culture were finally heard. In the United States, years of lobbying saw the passage of the Native American Graves Protection and Repatriation Act and the establishment of the Smithsonian National Museum of the American Indian. In Canada, protests resulted in a Task Force on Museums and the First Peoples. The recommendations of the task force grew out the recognition that it was "crucial that all stakeholders have full opportunity to express their views and exchange ideas."[4] Native people wished to be consulted and involved in telling their stories. The desire for such collaborations has resulted in substantial changes of museum practices.

My own dialogue with the collectors Charlotte Mittler, Elders Geronima Cruz Montoya, Ramoncita Sandoval, and Tony Reyna as well as community members and an advisory board of contemporary Native American artists, tremendously influenced the exhibition that was eventually presented in the Wheelwright Museum's gallery spaces. The exhibition consisted of nearly one hundred paintings. Seventy-seven paintings were by the students who attended the Santa Fe Indian School between the years of 1918 and 1945 and instructed by Dorothy Dunn. In the Slater Gallery hung fifteen works by the self-taught painters of San Ildenfso, who were painting at the same time that the earliest paintings by Santa Fe Indian School students were being created in the living room of the superintendent, John DeHuff, and his wife, Elizabeth DeHuff.

The Charlotte Mittler collection spans more than eighty years of Native American painting and is perhaps one of the most extensive private collections of this material. Mittler began her collection in the 1990s. Today her collection from this period of early Native American easel painting consists largely of works depicting dances and ceremonials, while other works are based on memories of the student's home life, such as herding sheep or plastering the abode home.

The fact that much of the collection consisted of ceremonial scenes was a little disconcerting for me. As a person from the northern prairie who was not privy to the Southwest's indigenous peoples protocol, I was cautious. For me, there is also concern that communities vary in terms of the degree of disclosure that is permissible regarding their spiritual practices. And to an indigenous person there is also the recognition that even in those seemingly benign depictions of everyday life are elements of ceremony and sacredness.

The pueblos of the Southwest have a long history in terms of their openness to outsiders, as seen in invitations extended to non-community members to attend annual feast days. Although outsiders are invited to witness the public portions of these communal prayers, there are spiritual practices that are not to be shared. Not being from a pueblo community, I was not certain that any of the subject matter of the student's paintings was meant for public viewing, although the paintings created by the students were meant to be sold and often visitors to the Santa Fe Indian School came especially to purchase work by the students. Times do change, and so do attitudes regarding past practices.

Before my selection as the curator of the exhibition, Charlotte Mittler organized an advisory group of contemporary Native American artists and community members. The group included Tony Abeyta, Rachel Agoyo, Mark Bahti, Gail Bird, Richard M. Howard, Yazzie Johnson, and Emmi Whitehorse. Out of these early meetings, the advisory group recommended that the curator for this exhibition be of Native American descent. Upon being hired, I met with the advisory group twice, and these discussions informed the thematic organization of the paintings in the main gallery.

Early in the project, the elders Geronima Cruz Montoya, Ramoncita Sandoval, and Tony Reyna Sr. were invited to view the collection with the specific intent to advise me regarding the paintings that could be shown publicly. Geronima Cruz Montoya is a graduate of the Santa Fe Indian School's studio program. Many of these paintings in the collection were created by Cruz Montoya's contemporaries and later her students. She was the instructor Dorothy Dunn's assistant and took over the studio program when Dunn left in 1937. Cruz Montoya remained in charge of the program until 1962. Ramoncita Sandoval is Geronima Cruz Montoya's younger sister and a graduate of the Santa

Fe Indian School. Tony Reyna (Taos) is a respected elder who also attended the Santa Fe Indian School with many of the students whose works are included in the collection. They shared stories of their experiences as students at the boarding school and insight into the lives of their classmates.

Paintings I thought would have been questionable did not receive the same reaction from these elders, which was surprising to me. However, taking into consideration their words and my knowledge of community taboos, as expressed by other community members, there were paintings that were not chosen for the exhibition or for publication in the catalogue. Many of these decisions were based on whether the subject matter would be seen by a member of the public if they attended the ceremony or activity. In some instances, this had to be negotiated between the collector, Jonathan Batkin (director of the Wheelwright Museum), and myself. At the end of the process, one hundred paintings were hung in the main gallery of the museum, and more than three hundred were printed in the exhibition catalogue.

Although the Indian School artists were physically absent from their communities, the imagery they created expressed memories of home with amazing accuracy and attention to detail. For viewers who share a common tribal affiliation with the artists, the paintings reaffirmed a collective history. One of the most difficult aspects of curating the exhibition and writing the catalogue for me was placing these works into a context that acknowledged the subject matter of the student's paintings while not diminishing or threatening the integrity of the spiritual practices or beliefs of their communities.

It was for this reason that I spoke to community members about the paintings, and in particular what it meant for them to view the works of these young artists, who may have been their mother, father, aunt, uncle, or grandparent. Often the words and thoughts these people shared spoke to notions of continuity, change, and community. My explanation of Lorencita Atencio's "Taking Lunch to the Ditch Cleaners" was a complex story of how gender and generational roles foster the realization of common goals within the pueblo.

The catalogue essay became much richer by including the words of Lorencita's son, Mike Bird Romero, who spoke of his own memories of the annual activity:

> The men would gather at the head gates and start digging.
> My Grandmother would cook all kinds of food for the
> men. All the ladies of the village would cook—it was ex-
> pected of them. Then at lunch they would gather the food
> into stacking pots, and along with the children the women
> would bring the food to them. The women dressed in
> traditional clothing. . . . I remember the men and women

Lorencita Atencio (T'o Pove), *Taking Lunch to the Ditch Cleaners*, 1936, gouache, 18 x 24 in. (47.5 x 61 cm.), Charlotte G. Mittler Collection. Courtesy of the Wheelwright Museum of the American Indian. Photograph by Mittler Photography.

would tease each other, with the men joking about how hungry they were and the women would tease and joke with them. It was wonderful. It was hard work because they would work twelve foot sections at a time, the ditch had to be six deep and three feet wide. And they would measure it with planks and if it fell short, you had to stay and dig until it was done. It was a community effort. When I think of those times I have a sense of belonging somewhere. No one went hungry, you had a place to sleep and clothes to wear and everyone helped each other.[5]

Another example is the painting by Harrison Begay titled "Navajo Weavers," in which the representational and abstract elements are combined to create a very complex narrative. The painting shows three women demonstrating stages in the process of weaving a rug. As the contemporary Diné weaver D. Y. Begay explains, the presence of the guardian figure references Diné ceremonialism. It is an image that recalls the origins of weaving and the oral tradition in which the Diné received the knowledge of weaving from Grandmother Spider.[6] The stories community members shared provided enough information to put the subject matter into a personal or cultural context while also demonstrating the complexity of these works of art.

I wanted this complexity to be reflected in the exhibition space. Paintings by the Santa Fe Indian School Studio students were exhibited throughout the United States and Europe over the years. The display of the paintings in these contexts was very standardized, often hung salon-style from floor to ceiling and grouped according to subject matter. Today, salon-style display is rarely used, but grouping according to subject matter is a practice that continues. My intent was to create a narrative in the gallery space that spoke to a more indigenous worldview, one that acknowledged the role of the seasons and cycles that dictated life and organized activities in our communities. To this end, paintings of fall ceremonial dances were grouped with paintings of other activities that occurred during that same time of year. The use of salon style was a compromise between the collector's desire to include as many paintings in the exhibition as possible, and my goal to create an experience that would not overwhelm the viewer visually.

This was my first exhibition as a curator, and in retrospect there are things I would have changed. It was the generosity of the indigenous community members and their willingness to share their insights that helped me present the work in a way that reflected an indigenous understanding and methodology.

Today we continue to bring indigenous methodologies and practices into our museum studies curriculum. It is through our encounters with students in the classroom that we refine these ideas as we put them into practice. The practices of mentoring and consultation are not new to indigenous people, but we are applying them to new situations. Whether we are working with a tribal community, a group of artists, or an individual, our objective is to give them the opportunity to express their views and voice their ideas.

AUTHOR BIOGRAPHY

Michelle McGeough received her MA in art history from Carleton University, Ottawa, with a specialization in aboriginal art. She holds an AA from the Institute of American Indian Arts in Santa Fe, a BFA and diploma in media arts from the Emily Carr Institute of Art and Design, Vancouver, and a BEd from the University of Alberta, Edmonton. McGeough was an assistant curator at the Wheelwright Museum from 2005 to 2010. She is currently the head of the museum studies department at the Institute of American Indian Arts.

NOTES

1   The American Indian Curatorial Practice symposium proceedings, "Visiting: Conversations on Curatorial Practice and Native North American Art," http://www.nancymariesmithlo.com/aicp_menu.htm.

2 Institute of American Indian Arts museum studies department review, May 4, 2005, 3.

3 Ibid.

4 David W. Penney, "Reflections on the Task Force," *Museum Anthropology* 16, no. 2 (2008): 10.

5 Michelle McGeough, *Through Their Eyes: Indian Painting in Santa Fe, 1918–1945* (Santa Fe: Wheelwright Museum of the American Indian), 47.

6 Ibid., 69.

This Place Called Home
Curating from an Insider's Perspective

Miles R. Miller

As a young boy, accompanied by my family, I joined the Washat religion at an area longhouse. I was nurtured with a traditional education; the elders taught me the Yakama legends and time-honored lessons, and encouraged me to understand everything around me. These early influences continue to inspire me as a beadwork artist. I learned patience, observation, design, and composition, skills that carried over to my collection management work. I learned to care for collections by thoroughly evaluating, completing, and updating accession and catalog records, thus facilitating the process of preservation and attending to exhibition concerns with care. The combined influences of my traditional Yakama upbringing, museology, and contemporary Native American art history studies motivate me as a curator to utilize exhibits as a new pedagogical method of pursuing Native American history, culture, and arts.

This essay will introduce the reader to *This Place Called Home*, an exhibit I curated in 2008 as part of my master's thesis project at the University of Washington's Burke Museum of Natural History and Culture.[1] In this essay, I will reflect on my experiences as a Native curator from the Yakama Nation—specifically how, in my opinion, traditional cultural beliefs enhance current museological practices and the relative power of decision making in collaborative projects between museums and tribal communities. Related to this shared management process, I will address two additional issues: (1) the relationship between pan-tribal

Guest curator Miles R. Miller (Yakama) with a 1988 capote (cat. no. 1988-119/1) made by Maynard Lavadour White Owl (Nez Perce/Cayuse), on display in the 2008 Burke Museum of Natural History and Culture exhibit *This Place Called Home.* Courtesy of the Burke Museum of Natural History and Culture. Photograph by Doug McTavish.

advisory committees and tribally specific values, and (2) possible tensions between culture and religion in museological practices.

In the course of the object-selection process for *This Place Called Home (TPCH)*, an Umatilla cultural adviser brought his concern over ten historical objects that might possibly fall under the Native American Graves Protection and Repatriation Act (NAGPRA) to the attention of

the Plateau exhibit curators. These archaeological objects come from
a particular accession in which the archaeologist and collector often
acted without the guidance and advice of local Native American con-
sultants. The intended use of these objects—a sinker/maul, sculpture/
effigy, pestle, ground stone tools, and stone mortars—is often mis-
understood. My course of action to resolve the issue was to research
accession records in search of evidence supporting this claim of a burial
connection. Finding no evidence, and acting as a curator familiar with
traditional Yakama teachings, I chose to override the recommendation
of the Umatilla cultural adviser. This internal decision making is indica-
tive of new understandings of what we mean by indigenous museum
curating and the implications of consultation.

THIS PLACE CALLED HOME

In March 2007 I accepted the invitation by Dr. James Nason, curator emeritus at the Burke Museum of Natural History and Culture in
Seattle, to cocurate a complementary, object-based exhibit to augment
Peoples of the Plateau: The Indian Photographs of Lee Moorhouse, 1898–1915,
a traveling photographic exhibition from the National Cowboy &
Western Heritage Museum.[2] Both *TPCH* and the Moorhouse exhibit
were designed to focus on the arts and culture of middle Columbia
Plateau tribes—Yakama, Umatilla, and Nez Perce—and as such, would
be the first major exhibits about Plateau culture in the past twenty years
at the Burke Museum.

The Moorhouse exhibit included fifty-one important historical
images of known people, village sites, clothing, and other objects of
material culture—all reproductions of Lee Moorhouse's glass plate
negatives taken at the turn of the century. The Burke Museum was interested in enhancing the exhibit to highlight and present to western
Washington audiences Plateau objects from the Native American permanent collection.

TPCH explored the indigenous aesthetic of the Columbia River
Plateau region. Carefully selected objects looked at relevant historical
and prehistorical objects characteristic of Plateau culture from the
Burke Museum, and demonstrated how the Columbia River Plateau
people visually represent a multidimensional and interdependent link
to their homeland.

My role as cocurator was as a museology student, a collection
manger, and a Yakama tribal member who happens to be a beadwork
artist. *TPCH* was my master's thesis project. I entered the assignment
wondering how best to signify eastern Washington's Plateau culture
given the insufficient funding that limited me to objects from the Burke
Museum's permanent collection. Borrowing objects from other institutions was out of the question, there were not enough resources to

purchase new objects, and requests for corporate or even tribal funding were denied. But these limitations, combined with concerns over culturally sensitive objects, became a motivating factor. I was determined to pull this exhibit together.

As a museology student, I began the University of Washington's museum studies program as an experienced collection manager with a burgeoning interest in curatorial work. Accepting the exhibit as my master's thesis project meant that I needed to impress on my thesis committee, the University of Washington, and the Yakama Nation that my experience and cultural knowledge combined to help me curate a successful exhibit on Plateau arts and culture. My previous work in collection management included many duties—one of which was to evaluate and write condition reports on objects selected for exhibitions use, noting whether the object was exhibit-worthy. The condition of each object was first and foremost in my mind. Each object displayed needed to be in stable condition, aesthetically agreeable, and culturally appropriate.

The lead curator, cultural advisers, and I were expected to make our recommendations in the object-selection process. The cultural advisers were given digital images and a report of each object. Being on-site at the museum, I had the advantage of examining and handling the actual objects in collection storage. Upon object review, several pieces were pulled immediately for failing to meet the previously mentioned prerequisites. For example, a particular cloth dress was removed due to the age, fragility, and unstable nature of the silk ribbon sewn onto it, and a pair of moccasins was pulled because they originated from the Northern Plains. A noteworthy discovery I made was that of a beaded vest, pictured in the *Peoples of the Plateau* catalogue, worn by One-Pie-High, a noted Indian war dancer.[3]

As a Yakama person, my fondest childhood memories are of when I would listen to and watch my Grandpa Joe and Aunt Rose tell our Yakama legends. They would animate each story by taking on the personality of various characters. These legends tell about the creation of landmarks or how animals received their markings. Grandpa Joe and Aunt Rose were fluent trilinguists who spoke the Yakama, Nez Perce, and English languages. Their lesson was twofold: to listen to and learn the Yakama language as well as to learn the moral of the legend. English may be my only language today, but I do remember the legends warmheartedly. Aunt Rose's favorite legend to tell was "The Origin of Basket Weaving." It is about a young girl who learned how to weave watertight, coiled cedar-root baskets, also known as Klickitat baskets. After completing her first basket, she is taught by nature how to decorate the baskets—the diamond comes from the rattlesnake, the stepped pyramid represents the mountain, and the stars, too, are symbolized in the basket designs. Alone these are simple geometric patterns, but put together in certain configurations they signify fishnets and migrating geese, quail, and salmon. These visual representations are still woven into the baskets and twined bags of the traditional Plateau artists.

As a boy listening to the Yakama legends, unique ephemeral images were stored within my memory. I grew up surrounded by traditional Plateau clothing, coiled cedar-root baskets, and twined bags decorated with customary Plateau designs. For twenty-eight years, I have been a beadwork artist, and my childhood pictures have combined with the traditional Yakama patterns to motivate me to create time-honored, inspired designs in a contemporary fashion. My keen eye for detail and experience help me to understand the tangible and poignant moment in time involved in both the creation of traditional and contemporary art and the practice of museology.

RELATIVE POWER OF DECISION MAKING

For successful collaborative exhibit projects between museums and tribal communities to work, the lead curators should define the original concept of an exhibit (the thesis or main point to be interpreted), create a list of proposed objects, and establish the composition and role of a cultural advisory committee. The advisory committee is a relatively new development for museum practice, introduced in the last twenty years of advocacy for Native rights in museums. Some of these developments are related to the passage of legislative acts such as the NAGPRA.

Native American tribes have a deep and enduring relationship to the environment, which is expressed in their traditional material culture, religion, and storytelling practices. Traditional culture thrives today due to the nurturance of stories that are carried by individuals responsible for their continuance. These community experts serve as curators not only in an object-centered sense, but also in a broader philosophical sense within their tribal contexts. They thus curate not only objects, but also deep spiritual knowledge. This spiritual knowledge highlights notions of ownership and use. As culturally sanctioned experts, the advisory committee members are also arbiters of the objects' proper use and interpretation.

The Burke Museum has an active Native American Advisory Board (NAAB) that, on behalf of the Washington State tribes, oversees the implementation of care for its ethnographic collections. The museum staff and cultural advisers brought together for *TPCH* comprised Comanche, Yakama, Umatilla, and Nez Perce tribal members. Each possessed knowledge of, or practiced, the traditional arts and culture of the Plateau people. Although the cultural advisers for *TPCH* were a separate working group from the NAAB, as cocurator I worked with the three cultural advisers representing the Yakama, Umatilla, and Nez Perce nations while Dr. Nason, the lead curator, worked with the Burke Museum's NAAB.

In preparation for the selection process, I reviewed and compared the images of *Peoples of the Plateau* to the initial *TPCH* list of ninety-nine objects selected by Dr. Nason. I developed a list that included the following criteria for selection of objects to be included: (1) Plateau—objects must be affiliated with the Yakama, Umatilla, or Nez Perce tribes; (2) condition—objects must be in stable condition, meaning they must be able to last the extent of exhibit, and withstand exhibit lighting and possibly cleaning; (3) exhibit history—objects must not have been previously exhibited or published; (4) aesthetic quality; (5) date; and (6) artist, if known. After meticulous research of the Plateau collection, I added twenty-four additional objects to broaden the list to 123 items.

The implementation of this exhibit was a shared experience between the curators and the cultural advisers, but discrete steps needed to be taken as well. Among the curatorial team there appeared to be an understood level of trust in my knowledge of traditional Plateau culture and my authorship of the exhibit's main theme. Using the criteria I established, I was asked to select the final objects and develop the exhibit story line in more detail. My curatorial statement read as follows:

> This exhibition expresses the rich traditional cultural continuity of my people—the Yakama, Nez Perce, and Umatilla. It also demonstrates how we see, understand, and represent our families, our homes, and world around us. Each of us perceives home differently. It can be represented by the gathering of natural foods, the ability to speak and understand our native language, or the way we see our land—from the sagebrush covered hills to the high alpine forests to the river banks of the Columbia River.
>
> For thousands of years Plateau artists incorporated geometric designs into stone carvings and rock wall paintings recording how they experienced and understood nature—especially the relationship between humans and the natural world. Today these distinct recognized patterns are symbols of place that connect us to our culture, history, environment, knowledge, and values.
>
> Present-day Plateau artists are inspired by and continue to use these symbols to identify tribal and familial backgrounds. Floral and pictorial images have also been incorporated. Drawing on oral histories, tribal celebrations, and landscapes, Plateau artists are creating remarkable new visual memories of this place called home.[4]

Ultimately, the exhibit encompassed clothing, archaeology, horse gear, and a DVD of modern-day artists and cultural specialists that explains to the viewer how the Plateau people visually expressed their relationship to their homeland.[5] I selected the objects, created the curatorial statement, authored the exhibit text and individual object label copy, and acted as liaison between the museum and the tribes in the selection of the community experts. The design elements were created with input from the curators and an exhibit designer. Consultation with the cultural advisers was necessary throughout the entire process for their input on object selection and label copy content, and their recommendations of artists for public programming events.

IDENTIFYING AND DEALING WITH DIVISIVE ISSUES

The combined influences of a traditional Yakama upbringing with studies in contemporary Native American art history and museology continue to inspire me as a practicing artist specializing in beadwork. I learned to pay attention to detail, a skill that carried over to my collection management work. This awareness of my people's practices is complemented by education and training received by studying and working at various mainstream educational institutions, including the Institute of American Indian Arts, the Smithsonian Institution, and Harvard's Peabody Museum. A combination of lived experience and formal training enhanced the work I pursued as a curator. For example, my familiarity with Columbia Plateau arts helped me to identify previously unidentified or unaffiliated objects as Plateau.

As a member of the Yakama Nation, taught to appreciate and respect traditional Yakama beliefs, I understand the importance of NAGPRA and Native American ethnographic museum collections. The issue of NAGPRA arose when it was discovered that several objects on the initial list were identified as culturally sensitive or burial related. I had prior knowledge of the objects' culturally sensitive identification, but since Dr. Nason previously selected these, I left them on the list. In the process of object selection, a member of the consultation team recommended that several archaeological objects be pulled. These objects included a sinker and maul, mortar, and other stone tools.

The cultural advisers for *TPCH* comprised Comanche, Yakama, Umatilla, and Nez Perce tribal members—a pan-tribal advisory committee focused on tribally specific values. The Plateau people, Yakama, Umatilla, and Nez Perce have overlapping or shared cultural beliefs: each speak related dialects of the Penutian language family, practice the Washat religion, and abide by similar unwritten laws of the Creator. Their ceremonies and material culture constitute the "heart knowledge"[6] that pays honor to a time long ago before there were people on this planet, when the animals were preparing the world for our coming. But there are distinct tribes and bands that make up these modern-day nations. The Yakama Nation alone includes fourteen tribes and bands whose semipermanent villages were scattered throughout eastern Washington. Although each tribe and band followed similar cultural beliefs, they had their own legends that told about the creation of landmarks or how animals received their markings.

The recommendation from one of the advisory team members to flag these archaeological objects in the database system as culturally sensitive sparked an internal discussion about power, legitimacy, and our mutual curatorial roles. I immediately researched accession records and other related documentation once this concern was brought to my attention. Could the two separate opinions—one that followed the original archaeological record, and my own, based on my cultural and professional training—be seen as a tension between religion and culture? I believe it was not necessarily the cultural or religious aspects of the objects in question, but more a doubting of my experience or cultural knowledge. It has been my experience at home to be told by an elder, "You are young; you don't know anything yet." I believe Dr. Nason recognized something in me that impressed him enough to ask me to cocurate. I also trust he felt I could settle the debate about the objects; if he sensed I could not settle this, he would have stepped in. He listened to me and reviewed my findings. Careful reviews of the object records found no evidence indicating a relationship of the archaeological material to burials.

In a September 11, 2007, letter, I wrote to the advisory committee that I felt comfortable keeping the selected objects in the exhibit:

> Though these objects [identified above] are from accessions that included funerary objects there is nothing in the records that would lead us to believe these objects are culturally sensitive objects. We greatly appreciate [your] diligent research in this matter. Dr. Bergen, collector of [the archaeological objects in question], often made assumptions in his notes about the use of objects; unfortunately, he did this without any tribal consultations or intimate knowledge of the culture. . . . I have carefully reviewed these object records and there is no evidence indicating a relationship to burials. . . . The other two cultural advisors involved with this project . . . have not expressed any concern over these objects. Following a discussion this morning with Laura Phillips, Archaeology Collections Manager, I feel comfortable with keeping these in the selection at least until I hear otherwise. . . . If you have any other specific information that you would

like us to consider about these objects, please do not hesi-
tate to contact the Burke.

I made the decision to override the cultural adviser based on my belief that archaeologists and collectors of the time rarely consulted with
tribes. The possible burial connection with the objects was made in
response to the accession record, which noted the collector's impres-
sion about the use of the objects in question. The assumption in his
notes about the use of objects was made without any tribal consultations or intimate knowledge of the culture.

Due to the age of the objects, their provenience is undetermined
even by tribal standards. I therefore allowed the ten archaeological objects that date between one hundred and nine thousand years old to
remain part of the selection process as evidence of the Plateau peoples
continued existence in this region. It was my understanding that similar
objects are on exhibit at tribal museums, which supported my decision
to have them displayed.

CONCLUSION

Throughout my life, my family encouraged me to balance an education in long-established Yakama philosophy with Western learning. As
a beadwork artist, I am continually inspired by and create traditional
Plateau designs in a contemporary fashion reminiscent of the historic twined bags, coiled cedar-root baskets, and clothing whose designs impart stories. The dramatic visual explanations I incorporated
into beaded bags, moccasins, medallions, and belt buckle patterns
are fragments of a longer story known only to me or to whomever received the finished product. This ancestry of experience of my people's
customs—heart knowledge, blood memory, and voice of the land[7]—is
complemented by education and training received by studying and
working at various institutions. I believe the combined influences of my
traditional Yakama upbringing, museology, and contemporary Native
American art history studies helps me to understand and respect the
material culture of America's indigenous peoples.

Curating a collaborative project such as *This Place Called Home* was
not only a testament of my knowledge, skills, and abilities as a curator,
but also evidence that the knowledge my elders taught me qualified
as cultural preservation standards. As a Native American in the museum field, I believe in joint projects between the museum, tribal communities, and Native American art historians in identifying object and
tribal affiliation, developing exhibitions, and creating new pedagogical
approaches to Native American history, culture, and arts. As a curator,
I believe in developing collaborative exhibition projects between museums and tribal communities, encouraging active participation of the

artists to articulate their tribal histories through visual dialogue, and inviting audiences to meet cultural specialists who can express their perspectives and experiences. As a collection manager, my interests are in evaluating and completing accession records, gathering, compiling, and updating provenances, dates, artists, and materials. I believe this type of partnership between varied constituents and practices is needed to strengthen relations between museums, tribal communities, and Native American art historians.

AUTHOR BIOGRAPHY

Miles R. Miller was born and raised in the Yakima Valley. As a beadwork artist, he creates traditional-inspired designs in a contemporary fashion. His beadwork has been exhibited at the Columbia Center for the Arts, Hood River, Oregon, and at the Museum of Contemporary Native Arts, Santa Fe, New Mexico. He earned a master's degree in museology from the University of Washington, a bachelor's degree from Evergreen State College, and an associate's degree at the Institute of American Indian Arts in museum studies. He curated *Lasting Heritage* for the Northwest Museum of Arts & Culture and cocurated *This Place Called Home* at the Burke Museum of Natural History and Culture. In 2007 Miller participated as curator's assistant with *The Requickening Project* during the Fifty-Second International Venice Biennale. His publications have appeared in various journals.

NOTES

1 Miles R. Miller, "This Place Called Home: A Columbia Plateau Arts and Culture Exhibit and Study Guide" (master's thesis, University of Washington, 2008).

2 For more information on these two exhibits, please visit the University of Washington's Burke Museum Web site at http://www .burkemuseum.org/static/plateau_arts/tpch/index.php and http:// www.burkemuseum.org/static/plateau_arts/moorhouse/index .php.

3 Miller, "This Place Called Home," 194.

4 See the full statement at http:// www.burkemuseum.org/static/ plateau_arts/tpch/about.php.

5 Miller, "This Place Called Home."

6 Leilani Holmes, "Heart Knowledge, Blood Memory, and the Voice of the Land: Implications of Research Among Hawaiian Elders," in *Indigenous Knowledges in Global Contexts: Multiple Readings of Our World*, ed. George J. Sefa Dei, Budd L. Hall, and Dorothy Goldin Rosenberg (Toronto: University of Toronto Press, 2000), 40.

7 Ibid., 46.

Moving Beyond the Expected
Representation and Presence in a Contemporary Native Arts Museum

John Paul Rangel

This essay is a critical ethnography of Native art and representation in a contemporary museum, the Museum of Contemporary Native Arts (MoCNA) in Santa Fe, New Mexico. I explore how one museum promotes and encourages the recognition of Indigenous ways of knowing, Indigenous models of representation, Indigenous aesthetics, and the delivery of knowledge pertaining to Native arts and culture. Intrinsic to this discussion is naming dominant cultural perceptions that are outdated, and intervening with decolonizing methodologies and Tribal Critical Race Theory (TribalCrit). Additionally, I elaborate on the ongoing discussion of Indigenous aesthetics by briefly surveying the 2009 traveling MoCNA exhibition curated by Ryan Rice titled *Scout's Honour,* featuring the work of Frank Shebageget and Michael Belmore, both Ojibwe from Thunderbay, Ontario.[1]

Native art, or what some still refer to as "Indian art," is commonly associated with silver and turquoise, dream catchers, objects adorned with beads and feathers, or pottery and textiles, particularly Navajo rugs and other "crafts." In commercialized settings, these objects are commoditized, fetishized, and romanticized abstractions of Native arts and culture, serving the consumers who buy them. When Native art and culture is displayed and represented in public institutions, such as museums, it is often packaged, presented, and consumed through the lens of the dominant culture, creating an imagined past where Native peoples are static, immutable parts of colonial history and conquest.[2]

Museums that display Native art using anthropological, ethnographic, and Western art historical models as interpretative lenses work to sublimate Native peoples and cultures into an imagined or romanticized past, creating an absence of authentic Native representations in the present. The museum, as a public institution and a producer and transmitter of culture and knowledge, is often one such site of sublimation and tokenization.

The Museum of Contemporary Native Arts, whose mission is the advancement of "discourse, knowledge and understanding of Native art,"[3] takes a different approach via their collection, exhibition, and interpretation of Native arts. The museum is a center within the Institute of American Indian Arts (IAIA), a federally chartered tribal college. As a Native-run "contemporary" art museum, MoCNA's ideologies and perspectives used to structure the exhibits, programming, and outreach efforts promote and encourage the recognition of Indigenous ways of knowing, Indigenous models of representation, and the delivery of knowledge pertaining to Native arts and culture. Indigenous ways of knowing include culturally distinct cosmologies, belief systems, values, traditions, and ideologies that are integrally tied to language, community, and place. Indigenous models of representation and the delivery of knowledge pertaining to Native arts and culture prioritize Indigenous ways of knowing over Western forms of representation.

There is very little written about contemporary Native art, Native art theory, or Native curatorial practice, and most of what is written is from a Western perspective. The number of books available by Native scholars about Native art and culture is disproportionally low compared to those written by non-Natives. This lack of scholarship is especially troubling given the prevalent stereotypical imagery and ideologies projected through popular culture, public institutions, and books that leave out or obscure the Native voice. These dominant cultural representations reify romanticized notions and naturalize racism. At worst, these images promote cultural and physical genocide.

Given this lack of resources, how are Indigenous perspectives conveyed in a contemporary Native arts museum? Native arts are often categorized into two main areas: "contemporary" and "traditional." This categorization is problematic, as it fictionalizes a fissure in cultural production instead of allowing for a more nuanced representation of a living, continual, thriving culture. Evaluating Native art through rubrics such as "contemporary" versus "traditional" forms static misnomers that force a distinction between an ahistorical "pre-contact" nostalgia and "post-reservation" cultural production. The dichotomous taxonomy of "traditional" and "contemporary" utilized in interpreting Native art results in a reductive privileging of the non-Native voice and authority on what constitutes the field. The Native museum is therefore tasked with a responsibility to cast off these reductive and constrictive binary models and reconceptualize what Native art is and means within a Native context. The Museum of Contemporary Native Arts uses the term "contemporary" strategically to assert a Native presence utilizing Indigenous perspectives and aesthetics to guide the production and display of contemporary art made by Native artists. This adoption of the conceptual framework "contemporary" is a major focus of my ongoing research at MoCNA and comparatively at other Native-run institutions. Contemporary, in this context, is employed to distinguish from the historical and ethnographic museums, which focus on and frame Native people and their cultures existing only in a romanticized pre-colonial, pre-civilization past. Contemporary means still existing today, producing art and contextualizing Native people and culture as part of the present and moving forward.

Located in the historic downtown arts district in Santa Fe, New Mexico, where the town's plaza is situated directly over an ancient Pueblo Indian village, MoCNA's architecture follows the adobe and wood Pueblo Revival style of the city, reflecting Indigenous and Spanish colonial architectural influences. This style was implemented to create a unified look and increase the city's aesthetic appeal as a tourist destination. Additionally, MoCNA inhabits a reclaimed federal building that has served historically as a post office and even a Los Alamos National Laboratory site. The physical attributes and the location of the museum are thus layered in contrasting identifications. A contemporary Native arts museum is in a U.S. government building that is near the center of a town that was built over a Pueblo Indian village. Over a few hundred years, Native Americans have symbolically reclaimed a small island of the lands they once occupied freely.

At this location for less than twenty years, the MoCNA has quickly become a prominent center for the production and display of contemporary Native art, especially since it is the only museum in the country solely dedicated to that endeavor. As one of a small number of museums focused on the display of and public access to Native art and cultures, this site is of vital importance to understanding Native representation. MoCNA has a collection of more than seven thousand contemporary works of art from more than 120 Native American nations, including paintings, sculpture, photography, drawings, prints, textiles, clothing, baskets, jewelry, pottery, ceramics, beadwork, and a small collection of historic material. The museum has an extensive collection of works by the faculty, students, and alumni of the Institute of American Indian Arts college collected since its inception in 1962. Additionally, the MoCNA, as part of the IAIA, provides opportunities for students and faculty to produce and display work in small temporary exhibitions.

The focus of the MoCNA is to present contemporary expressions of Native American arts and culture and to educate the public about the complexities of influence and cross-cultural exchanges, the prevalence of thriving Indigenous living cultures, and the ever-contested space of "identity." Identity, particularly for Native Americans, is a highly politicized sphere defined through the Indian Arts and Crafts Act of 1990. This act legally defines who is considered Indian and outlines the consequences for misrepresentation. While the act was theoretically initiated to protect Native artists, it in fact serves as a method of protecting the investments of Native art collectors. Legal definitions of authenticity imposed on Native artists and their implementations threaten an Indigenous reading of what constitutes membership in Indigenous communities.

As a contemporary Native arts museum located in a town and region where Native art is typically market-driven, MoCNA provides opportunities for the discussion of terms and phrases such as Native, American Indian, Indigenous, contemporary versus traditional, living cultures, and what is considered Indian art. The museum's staff of trained specialists (the director, chief curator, curator of collections, museum registrar, education coordinator, museum store director, graphic designer, special projects and community relations officer, and security/maintenance supervisor), many of whom are Native American, possess extensive knowledge and background on Native arts, archiving, and curatorial practice. The museum staff serve as ambassadors for Native America. This is yet another aspect of this institution that makes it such an important site for the transmission and representation of Native arts and culture.

CULTURAL THEORY AND ISSUES OF REPRESENTATION

Western frameworks that conflate Native arts and cultural production with Native crafts, artifacts, and material culture misrepresent the complexity of Indigenous cultures. Walter Benjamin articulates the methods through which Western representational frameworks replicate art in order to remove it from its originating context and, thereby, alter its significance and value.[4] The power to remove products of material culture from one specific context to another, as with cultural objects in an ethnographic museum exhibit, is an important tool for maintaining Euro-American hegemony. Euro-Americans define "Indian art" as "handmade" and then value it for this quality; thus "Indian-made" art is similarly valued because it is not mass-produced. Paradoxically, Euro-American popular culture can take a "Native object," and reproduce and distort it through the various machineries of print, film, digital, and synthetic manufacturing processes. This use of technology reduces the nuanced, distinct cultures such as the Haida, Cheyenne, or Apache to a generalized cultural signifier that becomes a symbol; through that process of reduction, the symbol comes to signify what Euro-America wants and needs it to signify. I argue that this type of reduction in Native arts and cultures becomes a simulation, silencing and erasing the originating cultures.

Similarly, Jean Baudrillard's characterizations of "simulation and simulacrum" draw on the reduction of art through mechanical reproduction.[5] Baudrillard posited that the original is replaced by a replicate or facsimile. The facsimile is a reduction of the original so that it can be usable and consumable. Euro-Americans create their version of "Indian" arts and culture, a simulation of the real and an absence of actual Native arts and cultural expression. In this regard, Baudrillard and Benjamin illustrate that the Euro-American simulation of the "Indian" is consumable, collectible, and not dependent on the original for context, authenticity, or meaning.

Native creative writers and literary critics have incorporated elements of Western cultural theory in their own work, appropriating and reframing it in order to construct Indigenous conceptual frameworks for the production and study of Native literature. Native authors Gerald Vizenor[6] and Phillip Deloria[7] examine the simulation and symbol of "Indian," to discuss what this term signifies and the erasure and eradication of Native culture(s) and identity(s), while simultaneously authenticating Euro-American national identity. Deloria traces the historiography of Euro-America's answer to its own postcolonial crisis, which was to essentialize an identity and claim to the North American continent through the appropriation of its version of "Indian" culture and tradition. Euro-America's quest for what it considered civilization prompted an alienation from nature as well as from a personal or national identity. To fill this void, Euro-America turned to Native American symbols to essentialize their identity (and culture). Native scholar Joanne Barker also examines the need for American "authenticity" as "preferring a retreat into nostalgia and transcendence from a modern, impersonal society through Indian beliefs that they believed connected them to a more authentic, natural truth."[8]

I argue that Euro-America has an ambivalent sense of national identity that is fabricated through the imagining of Euro-Americans as the originating and authentic peoples of the Americas by appropriating, and claiming as their own, interpretations and translations of various Native cultural signifiers. Co-opted in this way, these signifiers are corrupted, becoming distorted simulations of Native peoples from diverse nations and cultures. Barker points to the ideological problem inherent in Euro-America's relationship to Native America: "Indian-made art has made it possible, at least in part, not only to possess and own the Indian but to perform an Indian-ness that is personally and socially transformative. The contradictions within such practices form the foundation of a U.S. nationalism that has enacted a systematic dispossession and genocide of Indian people."[9]

Extending this concept further, Vizenor introduced terminology describing the structuring, naming, codifying, regulating, and surveillance that affect the mobility and agency of Native peoples. Vizenor identified an absence/presence paradigm, illustrated by a simulation he calls "Indian" and an absence of the "Native." By privileging simulation, the dominant culture can conveniently ignore and continually displace and dispossess actual Native people with living, thriving cultures. Vizenor intervened with the concept of "survivance," a combination of survival and resistance, and the concept of the "post-Indian," which I will return to later in my discussion of Tribal Critical Race Theory.[10]

NATIVE NORTH AMERICAN INDIAN ART AND INDIGENOUS AESTHETICS

A review of the texts on Native art and Indigenous aesthetics illustrate the need for Indigenous critical analysis and representation. Two surveys on Native North American Indian art provide familiar historical accounts of Native art, and trace the influence of contact on Native art and cultural production: Janet Berlo and Ruth Phillips's *Native North American Art*, and David Penney's *North American Indian Art*.[11] Both texts identify the need for stronger Native recognition and participation in the discourse on Native arts representation.

Berlo and Phillips wrote for mass appeal and to a non-Native audience. Their work draws from the canons of archeology and anthropology and focuses on works collected since contact. Their analysis of Indigenous belief, cosmology, spiritual value, symbolic power, and the gendered roles of art facilitate ways of understanding the visual culture of Native America that allow an evaluation of Indigenous art beyond typical Western aesthetic categories. Penney also utilizes the familiar territory of anthropological, archeological, and ethnographic representations of Native America based on regional geographic grouping.

Both Penney and Berlo and Phillips still privilege the voice of the non-Native author(s) above the narratives of actual Native scholars, artists, and art critics. Penney traced the continuum of native cultural production from pre-contact through the assimilatory periods to the near present, around the end of the last century. There is very little discussion of contemporary Native American art. Penney suggested in his closing statement, "Native Artists . . . have seized the apparatus of larger cultural discourse, the studio, the university, the gallery, the museum . . . but they are still represented primarily by museums specializing in Native American Art."[12] This limited scope of representation is problematic, as Native art is relegated to ethnic, historical, or folk art and is not recognized as having the same value and status as Western, dominant culture forms of contemporary art. The use of Western art categories is also problematic because of its inability to effectively analyze Native art, as evidenced in its systematic reduction, privileging, and silencing of Indigenous perspectives on art and aesthetics.[13]

The text *Indigenous Aesthetics: Native Art, Media, and Identity* uses a "systems approach" to Indigenous aesthetics. The author, Steven Leuthold, argues that artistic expression is interconnected with worldview, and that aesthetic experiences shape collective identity.[14] By complicating Western conceptions of art and aesthetics, Leuthold engages Indigenous artistic expression through spirituality, beauty, and ethics. This effort to construct a broader context for understanding and developing critical frameworks for Native art and cultural expression still lacks the inclusion of Indigenous narratives on arts, aesthetics, and cultural expression.

More recently, heather ahtone, a Native scholar, begins to define an "Indigenous aesthetic," identifying key signifiers that include the relationships between metaphors, symbols, cultural beliefs, knowledge, stories/histories, and personal narratives.[15] Metaphors and symbols connect stories, narratives, and culture intergenerationally, so that meaning and significance are preserved and renewed in what ahtone describes as "regeneration and reciprocity."[16]

As more Native scholarship is produced, there will be a greater understanding and recognition of Indigenous aesthetics. My own contribution to the analytical models described is that of connection to place, language, and the "Indigenization of space" as important signifiers. The Indigenization of space occurs when Native people reclaim a location through cultural signifiers, performance, ceremony, song, dance, or installation that convey the existence and presence of Native peoples and cultures.[17]

METHODOLOGICAL AND CONCEPTUAL FRAMEWORKS

Critical ethnography, as a methodological framework, functions well when looking at the production of knowledge and representation through a museum, an institution that historically has functioned as a hegemonic vehicle for the dominant society. Critical ethnography challenges the status quo and addresses issues of power, dominance, and inequality. In a description of ethnography, Creswell states, "Ethnography is appropriate if the needs are to describe how a cultural group works and to explore beliefs, language, behaviors, and issues of power, resistance, and dominance."[18] Additionally, critical ethnography intervenes in hegemonic discourse and provides a possibility for "critique and transformation of the conditions of oppressive and inequitable moral and social regulation."[19]

Before exploring how critical theory can productively be applied to Indigenous culture and arts, I want to be explicit about the dangers in assigning the frame of "Indigenous" to the diverse constituents known as "Native North America." As Native Americans are a minoritized group underrepresented in the academy, there is a need for more Indigenous research, and the development of a critical ethnographic framework is an appropriate intervention into Western discourse on Native representation. This grouping can be somewhat problematic, however, as Native Americans encompass a diversity of peoples, beliefs, and ways of knowing—distinctions that the dominant culture seeks to essentialize by categorizing distinctly different peoples with a multitude of experiences into one homogenous group.

There are certainly some commonalities shared by this cultural group. These include survival and persistence despite assimilation, genocide, restrictions on mobility and spiritual practice, and the decimation of sacred lands and ways of being. Also, historically, Native people are community-based and many have maintained aspects of their cultural distinctiveness, including language, spiritual practice, ways of knowing, and ecological connections to place. Often, Indigenous knowledge and cultural ways of being are not recognized, or they are marginalized and silenced by the dominant culture. Thinking beyond the Western circumscribed box requires both imagination and the revaluing of Indigenous conceptions of arts and culture.

Decolonizing methodologies and Tribal Critical Race Theory form a conceptual framework that creates a possibility for recognizing and validating Indigenous knowledge and perspectives on representation. Decolonizing methodologies acknowledge misrepresentation and seek to rectify issues related to Indigenous knowledge production and representation. TribalCrit names colonization as a key for understanding the imbalances of power relating to Native arts representation and knowledge production beyond the racial, ethnic, class, or gender issues normally addressed in Critical Race Theory.

Maori author Linda Tuhiwai Smith's *Decolonizing Methodologies* lays the groundwork for research and begins addressing the creation of Indigenous analytical frameworks for presenting Native visual culture.[20] Smith's analysis redresses the use of research for cultural colonialism and uncovers the imperialistic power structures that influence and guide the process of research. Smith outlines a methodology for Indigenous research and reeducation, which can be productive in working toward reclaiming historical documentation and the dissemination of information. Reclaiming and reeducating are critical for Indigenous peoples to exercise cultural sovereignty and self-determination. While the idea of the postcolonial is not applicable to Indigenous nations within the United States, Smith's methodologies function as a theoretical base for the redistribution of indigenous culture.

Critical Race Theory (CRT) also addresses these issues of power and inequality and begins to imagine interventions, resistance, and transformation. By Critical Race Theory, I mean the critical examination of the limitations of "objectivity, meritocracy, colorblindness, race neutrality and 'equal opportunity,'" which includes taking into account race, class, gender, and sexual orientation.[21] CRT challenges oppressive dominant ideologies by intervention, counter-storytelling, and analysis. Solorzano and Bernal suggest that group affiliation is important for social justice. That is, oppositional behavior and resistance address social justice when they move beyond the individual interest. For members of marginalized groups this includes having a "dual consciousness," which means acting from an awareness of the rules and expectations of the dominant society while also preserving and protecting the values, languages, cultures, and way of life intrinsic to their core identity.[22] Tribal Critical Race Theory (TribalCrit) similarly has the capacity to organize ideas around awareness and resistance in relation to Native art.

Bryan Brayboy asserts that TribalCrit is rooted in other disciplines, such as CRT, anthropology, American Indian studies, and education.[23] CRT and LatCrit address inequities based on race, gender, sex, and ethnicity in addition to class, however TribalCrit "emphasizes that colonization is endemic to society," a distinction that goes beyond a racialized theory of injustice to implicate Euro-American "thought, knowledge, and power structures" present in the dominant society within the United States.[24] In addition to the endemic nature of colonization, Brayboy observes that the dominant society has invested misconceptions of Native America. Further, Brayboy claims, Native people internalize and perpetuate these misconceptions when they fail to challenge them. MoCNA is situated in a geographic where Native people and culture collide with blatant misrepresentation and stereotypes that are constantly reinforced, reinvented, normalized, and marketed to the consumer tourist culture. Thus the prevalent forms of Native art are predicated by market and collector demands and expectations. TribalCrit is an important theory to begin to understand and conceptualize how a museum and its Native constituents of artists, academics, and administrators are intervening in a legacy of questionable and often offensive misrepresentation.

TribalCrit supports the recognition and use of Indigenous concepts of culture, knowledge, and power as important, where "culture" is described as being both "stable" and dynamic.[25] This conception of culture is significant in describing Native culture as being grounded but not immutable. TribalCrit is a useful way of looking at Indigenous aesthetics and representations that institutions such as MoCNA present as both an affirmation of an Indigenous presence and a desire to produce, define, display, and critique art and culture on their own terms.

INDIGENOUS PERSPECTIVES IN
A NATIVE ARTS MUSEUM

I return to my guiding question: how are Indigenous perspectives conveyed in a contemporary Native arts museum? Since the value-laden binaries of Western/Other and contemporary/traditional are so strongly present in both academic discourse and public perception, I am interrogating the subtleties and nuanced engagements of these terms within the culture of a Native museum where these dominant ideologies are either reified or challenged. Key to this discussion are the perceptions of Native arts and culture, transmission and reception, Indigenous perspectives, Indigenous aesthetics, and the (re)definition of Native arts.

Perceptions of Native America are difficult to change, particularly when there are investments toward romanticized, one-dimensional representations. The Museum of Contemporary Native Arts faces the challenge of educating the public, both Native and mainstream, about the kind of work the museum is doing and how it is unique. The internal perception among the administration and staff of the museum is that it is a diverse space. Tatiana Lomahaftewa-Singer, the MoCNA curator of collections, stated, "The museum is not tribally or regionally based, more of a national museum and contemporary, versus cultural. Other museums usually have the cultural art forms as the main exhibits and contemporary as a small focus, a room off to the side. This museum is the only museum that is dedicated to contemporary Native arts. If we do show cultural art forms, they are integrated into an exhibit and not segregated."[26]

I find Lomahaftewa-Singer's observations to be accurate. Her use of the term "cultural art forms" is a more productive way to imagine Native art beyond the familiar and ostracizing limitations of "contemporary" and "traditional." In Western art history, art is recognized and validated through canonical categories such as baroque, classical, surrealism, and primitivism. The terms "contemporary" and "traditional" reflect a Western art historical understanding of Native art. When Native art is categorized through this hegemonic lens, the entire body of Native art becomes a static, immutable entity, reifying the romanticized notions of a pre-historic, pre-contact, pre-civilization past—all dominant constructions in Western art history discourses.

Using a term like "cultural art form" can be useful in talking about Native art that is based on the reproduction of old or ancient designs, symbols, and iconography and often with materials that are tribally, culturally, regionally, or geographically specific (like clay from a particular place), but which can also include new influences (like the introduction of glass trade beads instead of porcupine quills). Lomahaftewa-

Singer also observed, "With cultural art forms, 'traditional' makes it sound like it is stuck and it can't grow, and that's not true. . . . Cultural art forms can include new materials and is a better way of describing what people refer to as traditional."[27] Additionally, contemporary Native people produce cultural art forms as a way of connecting to and preserving generations of creativity and tradition. This is something to bear in mind when analyzing ceramics, beadwork, parfleche, basketry, or powwow regalia; inherent in these forms are stories, songs, genealogies, oral histories, and indigenous aesthetics.

"Contemporary" Native art can be best described as an expression of values—personal, communal, or cultural—with attention to material conditions and current issues. The museum director, Patsy Phillips, credits the official conception of the institution (1962) and the earliest collection of works by students and faculty from IAIA as the actual inception of contemporary Native art.[28] Bradley Pecore, IAIA alumnus and museum educator, provided the following working definition of "contemporary": "Contemporary Native art is about 'values and not valuables,' to quote Mohawk scholar/IAIA instructor Stephen Fadden. The art is essentially reflecting the times and the values of the time. Right now this is contemporary, in a hundred years it will be called something else. This art now is reflecting the value systems of this particular society and culture. This is the visual, the self-expression, communal expression in some cases, that is happening today."[29]

Native art is essential, particularly for Native people, because the arts are integral to the expression of our living cultures. As Ryan Rice, chief curator, observes, "It's a continuum of our culture,"[30] succinctly situating the presence of the arts in Indigenous life. Tatiana Lomahaftewa-Singer elaborates:

> As Native people we have always understood, that when you do something, you have to do it well. One way is in the form of "art"—not just necessarily beauty and function, but it's a way of manifesting things that we believe in as well. We understand and value that those designs, techniques, and processes are important for carrying on our belief systems, our understandings of who we are that our ancestors and future generations are going to understand why those things came to be, why those things are there; it's a way of reaching out to what we cannot tangibly see, but that we know exists—art is also a way, an expression of what we think and believe in, what we feel.[31]

Connecting art and creativity to personal, communal, and cultural expressions is not a new concept; however, one of the biggest challenges facing those working on these issues is finding ways to teach the dominant culture to recognize that Native peoples have their own ways of interpreting and theorizing about who we are and what we do. Finding ways of communicating the authentic voice and experience of Native peoples, in this instance through the presentation of arts and culture, is a necessary undertaking. One example of how this can be achieved is the MoCNA's *Scout's Honour* exhibition.

Scout's Honour consists of various elements: rock, cloth, paper/prints, sheets of copper, and wooden objects. The installation uses mixed media with no recognizable cultural art forms (tribal or culturally specific marking, symbols, or materials). The pieces in this exhibit are uncontained and without physical barriers, which will allow people to interact with the artwork as opposed to simply observing Native "artifacts" through glass. The open display approach has been used in previous exhibits in this installation-based museum, distinguishing the MoCNA from other Native arts museums that rely on more traditional presentation methods (e.g., in cases and behind glass).

Frank Shebageget, an Anishinabe artist from Canada, incorporates the concept of multiples in his installation practice, and Michael Belmore, also an Anishinabe artist from the same region, is concerned with the environment and commodification. Chief Curator Ryan Rice noted that while the two artists originate from different reservations, both came from the same geographic region and through their art were responding to the changes they experienced and documented on a recent visit to their "home," which includes lakes, mountains, hunting/fishing areas, childhood residences, roads, rivers, and streams.

In the installation piece *Lodge,* Shebageget uses the de Havilland Beaver airplane to recall the introduction of this aircraft to the skies where he grew up. In a curatorial talk coinciding with the opening of the exhibit, Rice discussed the impact that aircraft like these had on Native lands, noting the pros and cons, such as noise pollution, greater mobility, and more contact with the rest of the world. Rice then displayed a picture of a beaver lodge native to that region, an image that becomes source material for this installation. Beaver plane multiples become a "beaver lodge." What followed were pictures of the 1692 miniature basswood replicas used in several configurations from previous exhibits. Rice commented that Shebageget was concerned with waste and sustainability in reference to the beaver lodge as a home from one perspective and a pile of sticks from another. Rice also described the exhibit as a "mapping exercise."

Here it is important to make distinctions between Indigenous mapping and colonial mapping. Colonial mapping is based on resources, property, and accumulation, while Indigenous mapping forges connections between language, culture, and place.[32] Indigenous mapping ties into indigenous aesthetics through the connections of people to culture,

Frank Shebageget, *Lodge*, 2008, basswood, gelatin, and steel, 90 x 50 in., collection of the artist. Courtesy of Frank Shebageget. Photograph by Scott Benesiinaabandan.

language, and place. Many Native artists, including Shebageget and Belmore, create from and reference those connections in their work.

Belmore's Indigenous mapping is influenced by his fascination with topography, communication, and technology. While showing images of Belmore's home landscape with its several unmaintained telephone poles, Rice explained in his curatorial presentation that telephone lines were no longer used since the area was becoming wireless like the urban areas. Rice also noted that the telephone poles were once great trees that came from the area and were returned "home," put to use, and then left standing but functionless. In the work *Snag*, ten silhouettes of telephone poles on small sheets of aluminum imitate these abandoned telephone poles. Rice indicated that the use of aluminum was intentional, as it is a synthetic material; Belmore's intent was to contrast the effect of humans on nature and the environment. Another example of Belmore's mapping is seen in the piece *Ridge*, an installation made of mosquito netting, hooks, and fishing line. The assemblage creates a "topographic map" of the watershed of his homelands. This indigenous mapping suggests connections to home, weather, water, sustainability, fishing, and protection against insects, namely mosquitoes, which are abundant near water.

Scout's Honour challenges the familiar notions of Native art; it is an exhibit of contemporary art produced by Native artists and conceptualized by a Native curator.[33] The installation challenges the viewer to think conceptually about the work without the comfort of being shown typical cultural art forms or recognizable "Indian" iconography. The exhibit strategies—installation, conceptual art, and interpretative data—advance the museum's mission of promoting dialogue and inquiry about Native presence.

CONCLUSION

I began this study with the examination of the westernized lens employed in the valuation and interpretation of Native arts, using critical ethnography and Western critical theory to unveil the ways in which these lenses become tools for co-optation and misrepresentation of Native arts. Decolonizing methodologies and TribalCrit theory form the conceptual framework that creates the possibility for moving past these limited hegemonic critiques. Decolonizing methodologies acknowledge misrepresentations and encourage movement toward a more inclusive research methodology within the academy, facilitating opportunities for Native scholars seeking to reclaim cultural, historical, and research patrimony. TribalCrit theory is an important interventional framework that has the opportunity to foster innovative discourses on Indigenous aesthetics, ones that supports Native conceptualized knowledge production, representation, and sites of resistance.

The Native presence in an institution such as the Museum of Contemporary Native Arts constitutes progress toward this larger project. The goal of the MoCNA is to increase visibility and awareness of Native arts beyond static, expected cultural art forms and interpretative approaches (historical, traditional, ceramics, jewelry, textiles, beadwork, etc.), and to encourage new discourses, both publicly and academically, about the current condition of Native peoples. Racism, commodification, the perpetuation of stereotypes, and romanticized notions of Native arts and culture still exist and continue to be reinforced, reproduced, and institutionalized. The counter-narratives and Indigenous representations displayed in this museum promote living peoples, thriving in distinctly diverse cultures, practicing tribal sovereignty, and producing indigenous knowledge.

The indigenization of space is particularly important, as it is the physical enactment of TribalCrit. The indigenization of space occurred when IAIA reclaimed the federal building that was built on lands once occupied by Native people. Similarly, it happens when a Native person alters a physical space, even temporarily, with installation art or images, song or dance, or a community meal and prayer. The Museum of Contemporary Native Art's effort to interpret and contextualize Native people and culture as being part of the present is an essential model of indigenous representation in the academy and the museum.

John Paul Rangel is of mixed race/ethnicity with Spanish/Mestizo/ Native American heritage and identifies primarily as a Native American. Rangel holds a BFA in studio art from the University of Texas, Austin, and an MA in American studies from the University of New Mexico. Currently, Rangel is a doctoral candidate at the University of New Mexico, where he is working on his dissertation on contemporary Native art. Professionally, Rangel has worked in several spheres of art creation and dissemination, from design and production to creative direction, marketing, public relations, and education.

N O T E S

1 The *Scout's Honour* exhibit was an "independent project" and traveling exhibition that Rice conceived and brought to MoCNA as an independent curator with no institutional affiliation. The exhibition toured to four venues: the University of Lethbridge Art Gallery, Lethbridge, Alberta; the Urban Shaman in Winnipeg, Manitoba; the Museum London, in London, Ontario; and MoCNA. Ryan Rice, personal communication, October 12, 2009.

2 I use Native or indigenous here to refer to peoples connected to land, place, ideology, language, culture, cosmology, and ways of knowing, particularly the domestically dependent nations within the United States. Indigenous also refers Native peoples to marginalized, disenfranchised nations globally.

3 See the Museum of Contemporary Native Arts Web site, http:// www.iaia.edu/museum/about/ missionmandatevision/.

4 Walter Benjamin, "The Work of Art in the Age of Mechanical Reproduction," in *Illuminations*, ed. Hannah Arendt (New York: Harcourt, Brace and World, 1968), 217–52.

5 Jean Baudrillard, *Jean Baudrillard: Selected Writings*, 2nd ed., ed. Mark Poster (Stanford: Stanford University Press, 2002).

6 See Gerald Vizenor's *Manifest Manners: Postindian Warriors of Survivance* (Hanover: Wesleyan University Press, 1994); and *Fugitive Poses: Native American Indian Scenes of Absence and Presence* (Lincoln: University of Nebraska Press, 2000).

7 Phillip Deloria, *Playing Indian* (New Haven: Yale University Press, 1998).

8 Joanne Barker, "Indian™ U.S.A.," *Wicazo Sa Review* 18, no. 1 (2003): 58.

9 Ibid.

10 Vizenor, *Manifest Manners*.

11 Janet Catherine Berlo and Ruth B. Phillips, *Native North American Art*, Oxford History of Art (Oxford: Oxford University Press, 1998); David W. Penney, *North American Indian Art* (New York: Thames and Hudson, 2004).

12 Penney, *North American Indian Art*, 212.

13 Emily Auger, "Looking at Native Art Through Western Art Categories: From the 'Highest' to the 'Lowest' Point of View," *Journal of Aesthetic Education* 34, no 2 (2000): 89–98.

14 Steven Leuthold, *Indigenous Aesthetics: Native Art, Media, and Identity* (Austin: University of Texas Press, 1998).

15 heather ahtone, "Designed to Last: Striving Toward an Indigenous American Aesthetic," *International Journal of the Arts in Society*, 4 no. 2 (2009): 373–85.

16 Ibid., 377.

17 John Paul Rangel, "Contemporary Native American (NDN) Art and Representation" (master's thesis, University of New Mexico, 2006).

18 John W. Creswell, *Qualitative Inquiry and Research Design: Choosing Among Five Approaches* (Thousand Oaks, Calif.: Sage, 2008), 70.

19 Roger I. Simon and Donald Dippo, "On Critical Ethnographic Work," *Anthropology and Education Quarterly*, 17, no. 4 (1986): 195–202.

20 Linda Tuhiwai Smith, *Decolonizing Methodologies: Research and Indigenous Peoples* (Dunedin: University of Otago Press, 1999).

21 Daniel G. Solorzano and Delgado Bernal, "Examining Transformational Resistance Through a Critical Race and LatCrit Theory Framework: Chicana and Chicano Students in an Urban Context," *Urban Education* 36 no. 3 (2001): 313.

22 W. E. B. Du Bois, *The Souls of Black Folk* (New York: New American Library, 1982).

23 Bryan McKinley Jones Brayboy, "Toward a Tribal Critical Race Theory in Education," *Urban Review* 37, no. 5 (2005): 425–46.

24 Ibid., 430.

25 Ibid., 434.

26 Tatiana Lomahaftewa-Singer, personal communication, October 12, 2009.

27 Ibid.

28 Patsy Phillips, personal communication, October 21, 2009.

29 Bradley Pecore, personal communication, November 11, 2009.

30 Ryan Rice, personal communication, October 12, 2009.

31 Lomahaftewa-Singer, personal communication, October 12, 2009.

32 A great example of this is Keith Basso's *Wisdom Sits in Places: Landscape and Language Among the Western Apache* (Albuquerque: University of New Mexico Press, 1996).

33 The works featured are part of the larger exhibit and referenced in the exhibition catalogue. See Ryan Rice, *Scout's Honour: Michael Belmore and Frank Shebageget*, ed. Paddy O'Brien (Lethbridge, Alberta: University of Lethbridge Art Gallery, 2008).

Unexpected Parallels
Commonalities between Native American and Outsider Arts

Dyani Reynolds-White Hawk

> "Otherances" tell more about the social and
> historical fantasies of the describers than about
> the people thus described.
>
> —*Paul Arnett, "An Introduction to Other Rivers"*

The fields of outsider art and Native American art, when compared with each other, provide discerning critiques of the ways that mainstream art institutions and their constituents tend to treat groups that have not historically been equal participants in the makeup of Western art history.[1] By mainstream institutions, I am referring largely to museums, galleries, and the academy that construct the prevailing value systems of the Western art world referenced as dominant in terms of power and prestige. My intent is to provide a broad analysis that complicates prevailing ideas about Native and outsider art in relationship to fine arts as a framework of reference. The comparative analysis of these polar fields will seek to identify repetitive behaviors of the mainstream art world in dealing with marginalized groups. Through the identification of similar patterns of treatment, we are able to reach an educated understanding of mainstream value systems applied to groups considered "other."

While my arguments may appear ambitious or overly generalized in terms of scope, I argue that a critical analysis of how Native and outsider arts are received has not to date been pursued in the literature.[2] Thus my explorations of these intersections may serve to introduce this comparative platform for consideration by future scholars engaging in specific case study analyses. My aim is to introduce readers to the complexities of outsider and Native arts reception, and to likewise assist viewers and artists in being equipped to tackle difficult issues such as race and bias while negotiating relationships between the peripheral and center in various arts worlds. As an artist and as a Native American trained in the higher education system, I am inescapably engaged in the challenging relationship between the fine art world and the Native American art world. In this essay, I am seeking to extract core issues and find evidence of some of the larger challenges that are presented in this relationship of Native Americans and the academy. The African American theologian Cornel West has stated, "I'm as much concerned with how we understand modernity and the dominant culture as with the African-American experience."[3] This statement parallels the motivations of this investigation, that through an understanding of the values of the mainstream art world, a greater understanding of self and community in relation to this entity can occur.

ESTABLISHING FOUNDATIONAL CHARACTERISTICS AND DIFFERENCES OF NATIVE AMERICAN AND OUTSIDER ARTS

The world of outsider arts, also referred to as self-taught, folk, or vernacular arts, is defined by the characteristics of its makers. It is not restricted to a particular geographic location, race, or national heritage. The artist's primary attribute is defined as a lack of formal training or credentials. Along with this lack of formal training, there is a perceived lack of influence by the field of art history and mainstream communities. Outsider arts are therefore perceived as pure, unadulterated, individualistic forms of innate expression, often falling into various classifications such as rural, poor, less educated, mentally ill or unstable, prisoners, homeless, or any variety of other combinations that socially set them apart from the median. Their otherness is "based more on sociological and psychological factors that are held together principally by commonly made claims by Outsider Art's apologists. . . . This difference is not merely marked by exclusion from the mainstream of the professional (western) art world, but also by exclusion from, or marginalization in relation to, the very culture that supports the market for mainstream art."[4] Thus, by the nature of its qualifications, outsider art can be practiced by anyone fitting the outsider criteria of any race, in any country. Although outsider art is not ethnically based, because of its focus on the biography of its makers, the field has been linked to the category of identity art.

Native American art, like that of any other culturally specific group, is similarly defined by the characteristics of the artist. Identity lies at the center of dialogues involving Native American arts. This identity issue is distinct from that of outsider arts on the grounds that in Native North American arts, political standing and nationhood define identity. There are 562 federally recognized tribes in the United States, with many more state-recognized tribes, and even more yet that remain unrecognized—as well as tribes throughout Canada. Each one of these tribes is an individual, sovereign nation with their own governing body, each dictating their own regulations regarding tribal membership. Further, Native American arts are the only racially defined category of arts in the United States with federal legislation regulating the authenticity of the practitioners involved in the market.[5] The Indian Arts and Crafts Act of 1990 makes it illegal to sell artwork promoted as Native American unless the artist is an enrolled member of a federally or state-recognized tribe or an officially certified Indian artisan recognized by a tribe. The history of this law dates back to the early 1900s, when mass-produced imitation Indian jewelry and goods first flooded the market. The Indian Arts and Crafts Act of 1990 was preceded by the passage of the New Mexico Indian Arts and Crafts Act in 1959 and the establishment of the federal Indian Arts and Crafts Board in 1935.

It is within these identity politics that outsider and Native American arts, having little to no affiliation with one another, are faced with similar challenges and, arguably, some advantages as well—such as readily available specialized markets. They are characteristically divergent groups—outsider artists as an unorganized body, dictated by individual biographies that are often viewed as a form of social oddity, and Native American arts as dictated by ancestry, a communal history, and a politically defined relationship with a tribal nation. Yet these two groups have historically been addressed very similarly within the realm of mainstream arts—as fleeting interests. Each are brought into mainstream institutions in a manner similar to what we would expect of an invited guest, at times even an honored guest. While we may exalt and care for a guest, when the visit is over, we expect them to leave, at which point our lives return to the comfort of what we know. Consider the following quotes regarding outsider and Native Arts respectively:

> Despite the lip service given to the "blurring of the lines"
> separating high and low art in art museums today, it is still

extraordinarily difficult for even the finest of vernacular or "self-taught" art to gain a permanent place in them.[6]

Ironically, the last to receive commercial and institutional attention in the urban artworlds have been the "first Americans," whose land and art have both been colonized and excluded from the realms of "high art," despite their cultures' profound contributions to it.[7]

Why would these distinctively unique groups be facing essentially the same treatment from the mainstream art world? One may expect to see such similarities when comparing various ethnic groups and their passages through academically centered art worlds. This seems commonsensical when considering that the white male has historically held a monopoly in academia. Outsider arts, however, cannot be defined by race.

To better understand the foundational issues informing these relationships and to define a base from which we can further investigate these questions, I highlight three primary ideas or focal points for discussion of both outsider and Native American art: (1) notions of nostalgia and romanticism; (2) concerns of authenticity; and (3) the buying of a story (biography) or the collection of culture. Although these categories are intimately intertwined, with the distinctions between them at times blurred, an examination of each discussion point yields productive findings. As imposed forms of regulation, these parallels evidence patterns of mainstream art institutions when dealing with groups historically excluded from Western art history.

NOTIONS OF NOSTALGIA
AND ROMANTICISM

> Nostalgia: a wistful or excessively sentimental
> yearning for return to or of some past period
> or irrecoverable condition . . . something that
> evokes nostalgia.
> —Merriam-Webster Online Dictionary

> Romantic: marked by the imaginative or emotional appeal of what is heroic, adventurous,
> remote, mysterious, or idealized.
> —Merriam-Webster Online Dictionary

Both outsider and Native arts are viewed as exotic, mysterious, not easily accessible, and something to be discovered. Moreover, they provide middle- and upper-class American society access to a near but unattainable notion of the past or a return to values more closely associated with the natural world, away from pretentious contemporary societal and historical art concerns. Consider the following comparable excerpts: first from Molly Mullin's *Culture in the Marketplace: Gender, Art, and Value in the American Southwest*, regarding the nation's largest annual Native American art market, the Santa Fe Indian Market; and second, similar concerns noted in Gary Fine's *Everyday Genius* regarding self-taught art:

> There is much going on at Indian Market that exhibits the characteristics of contemporary primitivism—recent manifestations of the expectation, common among the middle and upper classes throughout much of the last hundred years or so, that societies and things considered "primitive" can provide members of the supposedly more "advanced" societies an antidote for modern anxieties. The antidote includes a sense of wholeness, authenticity, purity, and harmony with nature.[8]

> Visiting Appalachia, and becoming friends with and patrons of the artists, helped guilt-ridden, educated bourgeois young Americans feel "a margin of escape" from their comfort and consumption. . . . For others, such as collector Chuck Rosenak, it was the surprise that an underclass existed: "Suddenly . . . I realized, really for the first time, that America was not just the affluent middle class. I mean, there were other people and these people had dreams and visions and ambitions and that this collectively made up an America that we knew nothing about, and had never read about, had never experienced. And so I set out . . . to find out what it was like in America."[9]

These groups are often considered apart from their viewing audiences and therefore not contributors to the ongoing intellectual dialogue characteristic of mainstream art concerns. Instead, their marginalized status provides notions of relief, a return to a sense of basics, instinct, intuition, innate creativity, and moreover, to a sense of culture. Outsider and Native arts provide an oasis from American mainstream art models, teasing their enthusiasts with purchased or "discovered" tokens of alternative worlds or cultures radically different from their own, while simultaneously promoting vintage American dreams. The lure is evidenced in the tourism associated with these fields, in which the tourist is seeking a romanticized foreign experience.

The American Southwest is a leading example of tourism based on the romantic sentiment of Native American culture. "A significant portion of the allure of the Southwest generally and Santa Fe specifically is built on a mystification of Native American cultures," writes Karl Hoerig. "Over the course of the past century, non-Indian people have come to the Southwest in droves, searching for the spirituality, the unity with the natural world, the exotic mysticism that visitors perceive in the lives of the Native people of the region."[10]

A factual account of Native American history and present life circumstances is widely unknown by non-Native Americans. What is generally known is a brief, subjective history provided by the public school system. This insufficient information is supported by fictionally based stereotypical images widespread in the media. The result is an overarching notion of a pan-Indian ideal frozen in the images of the late 1800s to early 1900s. As Hoerig suggests in the previous quote, the tourist population is seeking an experience based on ideas of this fictional image. They are looking for an interaction with a traditional past or a romanticized notion of a traditionally inspired spiritual present. Native American artwork, inescapably entwined with this history, becomes a tangible connection to these ideals in the mind of the cultural tourist/collector.

The art historians Janet Berlo and Ruth Phillips address the complicated history of Native American arts in tourism, explaining the paradoxical situation created by the desire to collect artwork that the cultural tourist expects to support the nostalgic definitions of the collected: "The modern trade in Native art turns on this aspect of doubleness. On the one hand, the market for Indian art grew in tandem with the entrenchment of assimilationism and the dogma of the Vanishing Indian. Yet, on the other hand, the commodity most desired by buyers . . . was 'Indianness' itself. . . . They romanticized the Indian as still connected to Nature and to local community, ties that many non-Natives believed to have been broken by urbanization and industrialization. Buyers of Native-made objects, whether 'crafts' or 'fine art,' sentimentalized and romanticized their acquisitions as precious traces of lost authenticity."[11] Many contemporary Native artists working today struggle with the side effects of this tourist market that instills patrons with preconceived romantic notions of what they believe "Indian art" should look like.

Outsider arts are similarly supported and defined by tourism, which produces a similar type of lived experience, providing the ultimate package deal—the artwork coupled with the exotic encounter. The opportunity to meet and speak with the artists, even possibly build a relationship, is of primary importance to many outsider art collectors. The transition from the "fetishizing of folk art objects to the fetishizing of the people who make them" has been described as a quest: "The successfully intimate interaction in the present—that one-on-one, face-to-face encounter with the non-alienated individual. . . . The artifact is no longer treasured as an end in itself . . . but merely as a clue to the true object of desire, the designing artist."[12]

A particularly curious example of outsider art tourism is the folk art homes tour, which provides collectors with an all-inclusive outsider art collecting experience, combining "elements of pilgrimage, weekend antiquing, safari hunting, and amateur ethnography."[13] This is a central form of tourism in outsider arts consumption, a trip by the consumers of outsider arts (dealers and collectors), to the artists' home environments. Both Gary Fine's and Suzanne Seriff's labels for these tourist encounters—"folk art quest" and "folk art adventure," respectively—provide indications of the intended goals. Carl Hammer, a Chicago-based outsider art dealer, illustrates the romantic notions of such an encounter, stating, "I always had these kind of Indiana Jones romanticized ideas of what I was doing, you know, driving my van through the South and kind of studying southern culture at the same time I'm doing this kind of collecting thing."[14]

The career of the iconic outsider artist Edgar Tolson reveals various forms of nostalgic attraction to outsider arts, such as a longing for an American past associated with preindustrial-era values, and an interest in the "primitive," "real life," and tradition. Tolson's earliest supporters were privileged college students whose prospective futures were likely to fall within academia, professional careers, or the military. Their encounters with Tolson provided an imagined alternative to these scripted futures through nostalgic notions of an innocent past: "For many admirers folk art represented freedom and the impunity of childhood. . . . In contrast with the intellectual reserve of much fine art and the special knowledge required to crack its code, folk art, through formal simplicity and, in some cases, awkwardness, seemed an invitation to reanimate the world through irrational and spontaneous play."[15]

Notions of nostalgia and romanticism associated with outsider and Native American art are elevated ideas about the existence of the other. Idealized traits are irrevocably bound to the concerns of authenticity—the validity of the out-group as real and genuine. These constructions are so pertinent that the value of these cultures and individuals is assessed by high expectations of originality and worth.

CONCERNS OF AUTHENTICITY

Outsider arts do not have federal legislation like that of Native arts regulating and defining its makers, but they certainly do come with their history of debates—namely, who and what qualifies as outsider. The authenticity of these artists lies first and foremost in the biography of the individual. Outsider artists usually live either physically or mentally on the outskirts of society. Their life histories generally hold stronger merit that the work alone. The work must be authenticated by the biography. There are many contemporary artists that appropriate stylistic conventions or imagery from outsider arts, but they are not considered outsider artists because of their active participation in mainstream fine art communities.

An active market has been created around outsider art, and with this comes the lure of individuals that feel they could benefit from association with outsider status. This phenomenon of appropriation or ethnic fraud closely resembles the misrepresentation of Native American arts: "A market niche exists, which these unsuccessful, but trained, contemporary artists are willing to fill. The boundary between folk and fine art must be policed on both sides of the border."[16] While the Indian Arts and Crafts Act literally polices the authenticity of Native American artists, no such parallel legislation exists to monitor the equivalent of ethnic fraud in outsider arts, yet policing is certainly practiced on an informal level by its patrons.

An example of the extreme difference expected in outsider arts is the case of the British artist Albert Louden. After defining himself as an outsider artist, he later began to sell his work in commercial galleries. Some of the dealers that bought and sold Louden's work previously no longer consider him an outsider: "He might as well be mainstream." Collectors expect of artists poverty, strange behaviors, and above all an "indifference to earning money."[17]

One of the more captivating notions of authenticity involving outsider and Native arts is the idea that the qualifying criteria are not set up entirely from within their own communities, but are defined primarily by the very cultures that view them as peripheral. This has been carried out in a variety of ways, including through the power of the economic market. What that market responds to, and therefore invests in, often serves as the strongest governing body of what is accepted as authentic within a category. If the market purchases only outsider art made by southern black Americans or only Native arts made by people living on reservations, then these characteristics become defining. The market's focus on difference results in an imposed restriction on how an artist is able to conduct not only their artistic practices but their lives as well.

In Native art circles it is often only the most traditional work that is highly regarded in the fine art circles and collections—works that are perceived to have been the least tainted by European influences. This limitation discredits a contemporary Native existence and contemporary Native arts and concerns. Many Native artists have produced a great deal of work confronting these issues. Their work leaves us with visually tangible evidence of the efforts to address stereotypical nostalgic and romantic misconceptions of Native life—and the public's expectation for these misconceptions to be reflected through Native arts. The contemporary Native artists Harry Fonseca and James Luna have utilized humor and reverse psychology to lure people into understanding the desire for an equal playing ground. For Fonseca, this has been materialized through his coyote or trickster imagery, an icon widely recognized as a character symbol of Native oral traditions.

Fonseca's coyotes serve as self-portraits and are found dressed in street clothes and contemporary dress in a variety of humorous scenarios. "Fonseca's coyote is able simultaneously to laugh at himself and at others," writes Peter Selz. "He embodies paradox and ambiguity and personifies the Native American as both separate from and a part of the dominant culture."[18] The use of the coyote places Fonseca's identity firmly within a Native tradition, literally embodying oral traditions. These coyotes exist within stories of a contemporary existence, donning leather jackets, dancing in modern establishments, and leading an urban existence. The coyote is a part of this modern story, yet inherently a part of a traditional story as well.

James Luna takes a more somber and direct approach to humor in his pivotal 1987 performance titled *The Artifact Piece.* In this work, he put himself on display lying on a bed of sand in a display case, wearing only a loincloth, at the ethnographic museum, Museum of Man, in San Diego. Two other display cases accompanied the performance case—one housing medicinal and ritual objects from his tribe and the other containing found objects from 1960s counterculture. Following *The Artifact Piece,* Luna created another performance piece for the Whitney Museum of Art, titled *Take a Picture with a Real Indian* (1991). Selz addresses this work in *Art of Engagement:* "This installation presented Luna, once again in a breechclout, next to cutout portraits of himself in traditional garb or in Western street clothes. Spectators were invited over a public address system to have their pictures taken with a living ethnographic artifact to show how fond they were of the Native population. The resulting photos, with museum visitors posed next to the live Indian artist, turned the humiliating photo op on its head: Who is the subject here?"[19]

Works such as these serve as vivid illustrations of the reactions of Native artists toward the history of America's general relationships with and ignorance of Indian cultures. They are reactions to the ways this lack of knowledge has trickled into the operations of the art world, often restricting Native arts into what the mainstream American public perceives as authentically Indian—a frozen image of the pre-contact Native American. While the economic market may appear to have a stranglehold on the reception of Native arts, other mainstream venues such as the museums that hosted Luna's performances have provided a platform for voices from Native American art communities to be heard. Ideas surrounding self-imposed or non-self-imposed concerns of authenticity have gained power through collective institutions such as tribal colleges, museums, galleries, academia, and scholarship.

Outsider artists, to my knowledge, have not collectively gathered in efforts to claim power over their own field deciding who could or could not be included. Many outsider artists don't even label themselves as artists until their works are "discovered" by individuals involved in mainstream art communities. As Colin Rhodes points out, "Compared with 'insider' movements in western art such as Impressionism or Cubism, which functioned in socially sophisticated ways, individual outsider creators seldom even know of each other, let alone form a cohesive group."[20] Organization as a collective may be viewed as problematic because active participation in their own careers and the workings of the art world are viewed as contradictory to the definition of outsider. The following quote from Fine provides insight into how these restrictions play out in the market: "Marketing can be a four-letter word. A dealer noted of one of her artists, 'He's very well-organized and has a color Xerox of all his paintings, and does duplicate paintings of some of them. . . . So, in a sense he's sort of commercialized himself. . . . I don't show people his color Xerox brochures, because I think that detracts from his authenticity. I think he is authentic, but I think it turned people off. . . . I don't think they should be really good at marketing themselves. I think it detracts from their authenticity [She laughs].' Career skills taught in art schools are counterproductive."[21]

Similar effects of identity politics run rampant in the field of Native arts, not only surrounding legal matters and blood quantum, but also concerning questions of authenticity linked to ideas of what is traditional versus contemporary Native art. Unanswered questions include problems such as: Is anything made by an Indian, Indian art? Does it need to have particular "Indian" physical characteristics or content for it to be authentic Indian art? Would a cubist painting done by Geronimo be Native art? What about a cubist painting done by a mixed-blood MFA student that was a descendent of Geronimo? What about traditional quillwork taught by an elderly Lakota woman to her adopted, non-Native grandson? Similar questions of authenticity regularly permeate the conversations in institutions such as the Institute of American Indian Arts and markets such as the Santa Fe Indian Market, exposing the lasting effects of imposed forms of colonial definition and the more positive ongoing efforts of self-determination.

BUYING A STORY, BIOGRAPHY, OR CULTURE

Minimally educated, fundamentalist, homeless, self-proclaimed expressionist, wood carver torn between religion, human temptations, illness, and family, prolific recluse, obsessive collector and creator without purpose beyond personal vision, preacher that paints because God told him to, mental hospital patient creating her own worlds of escape on paper, these are all examples of biographical stories of outsider artists. They are intriguing and appealing, as they exist outside the average American everyday experience.

In outsider arts, the biography plays such a central role that ongoing debates exist between those that believe the biography comes first and those that believe the work comes first. Given the movement of outsider arts into acceptance as fine arts in limited contexts, the emphasis on biography seems extreme. It contradicts everything taught in academic arts about the importance of the work itself, that contextual assessments should only complement an already independently exceptional piece.

One example that reinforces this point is the case of Mary Nohl, who studied at the School of the Art Institute of Chicago from 1933 to 1937, receiving a BFA. She pursued various avenues in the arts and even taught art from 1939 until 1946, when she opened her own pottery studio, which she ran until she lost interest in 1956. As the daughter of a successful lawyer, Nohl had the financial means to travel extensively, submit her work to various shows, and collect. Nohl actively studied the natural world and consciously derived influences from literature and her travels. Her full participation in a mainstream lifestyle would seemingly identify her as an arts insider, but in the 1960s, Nohl's life took a significant turn. In two years, she lost her brother, his wife, and her father. Soon afterward, her mother entered a nursing home, leaving Nohl for the first time alone in her family home in Fox Point, Wisconsin. From this point on, Nohl became a prolific, dedicated, and life-consuming environment builder. Her entire home was covered in her work, inside and out. Home repairs became art projects and her yard became a sculpture garden. Her life consisted of collecting whatever objects might serve as art materials, working on her projects and creating an all-inclusive, active, dynamic environment. The increasing attention garnered by her ever-growing art project prompted some neighbors to create stories about her, labeling her a witch. Others adored her work. She was both loved and feared in her community until her death in 2001.

Nohl's life serves as a prime example of an individual functioning fully within mainstream society and moreover within mainstream art practice—a lifestyle that would surely disqualify one as an authentic outsider artist. Yet she serves as an excellent example of what it means to function as an outsider artist. While the materials used (such as concrete and found objects) could serve as signifiers of an outsider art practice, her obsessive nature, somewhat reclusive behaviors, and biography signaled her complete inclusion into the world of outsider artists. Without these extreme characteristics, if her art stood alone, Nohl most certainly would not be considered an outsider.

Native American arts are dominated by the power of the artist's biography as well. During the Santa Fe Indian Market—a pillar in the world of Native arts, estimated to have generated over $100 million[22]—any visitor could easily walk through the crowd and pick up a range of stories being exchanged between artisan and potential buyer on the cultural history of their work. As with outsider art, these conversations serve as supporting material of biographical interest in the eyes of the collector.

Even today there are Native people at the Indian Market dressed in full traditional regalia selling photo opportunities to eager tourists, an ironic twist on James Luna's *Take a Picture with a Real Indian*. Many Native artists value the Indian Market and the opportunities it provides to share aspects of Native culture with those who are eager to learn. Considering the history of America and its tendency to hide or push aside Native history, the passionate student is refreshing and appropriately appreciated. On the other hand, some artists are very aware of the patterns of collecting culture and resent the exoticism that accompanies the Indian Market, viewed as the result of centuries of oppression that are dealt with in contemporary times in arenas such as the art market. Rick Hill, a Tuscarora artist, states, "There's a difference between culture and commerce, and Indians understand that really clearly. They understand that the purpose of Indian Market is to put as much of the white man's money into our pockets as possible. It's not to convert them about the truth of our existence, but to make an income. The non-Indian doesn't understand, because they think they are buying Indianness. They don't realize they can't buy that."[23]

Efforts by Native communities to both establish a voice honored by mainstream art institutions and exert power over their own artistic destiny have affected the desire of the consumer to control the circulation of Native arts. Aesthetics and biography are therefore similarly charged parameters of reception: "The decision by indigenous people to engage in the business of ethnic tourism is to accept encroachment from outsiders, but it does not necessarily signal a loss of agency."[24] Karl Hoerig's statement implies a conscious decision by Native artisans to actively engage in cultural exchange through tourism and sales.

While the values inherent in buying culture are generally well understood by Native artisans, it is less clear how these assumptions affect outsider arts. The beginnings of cultural tourism based on ideas of adventure and collection are prevalent in the field of outsider arts, signaling a useful comparative approach. The history of collecting Native arts is older than the history of collecting outsider arts, so perhaps these disparities simply mark an indication of what might transpire in the future. This is not to imply that outsider arts were not being produced at the same time as Native arts, but simply that their recognition as such and involvement with Western artistic traditions is considerably younger.

Charles Russell examines the occasional spotlight on outsider arts, calling them "token appearances." He argues that although the realm of self-taught art has occasionally garnered the recognition of these institutions of power, these moments of inclusion have not "challenged the concept of fine art, nor have they explained adequately just why the self-taught belonged in the shows." Russell explains that the art world, despite various moments of multicultural rhetoric throughout modernism, still maintains itself as a "privileged space. . . . Even as a pluralist vision acknowledges other aesthetic systems, the artworld continues to serve as an agent of cultural legitimation and sustains the class and market bound practices that eviscerate any meaningful challenge to that artworld."[25]

The exploration of the patterns of behavior or value systems of the mainstream institutions highlighted here are presented as tools for further exploration in the continued dialogues of these intertwined fields. Through such exploration of foundational understandings, we are better prepared to knowledgably work toward subsequent goals—whether these are more open-minded views of what is considered and included in these institutions as "art," or teaching emerging artists and art field participants of the challenges they may face. It is the artists themselves that must ultimately choose how they may deal with these intractable divides in their own practices.

AUTHOR BIOGRAPHY

Dyani Reynolds-White Hawk holds an MFA in studio arts from the University of Wisconsin, Madison, and is currently the Arts Project Manager at the Native American Community Development Institute in Minneapolis. She earned a BFA in two-dimensional arts from the Institute of American Indian Arts, where she recently exhibited in the Museum of Contemporary Native Art's *Soul Sister: Reimagining Kateri Tekakwitha*. Reynolds-White Hawk won the 2011 Best of Classification (Painting, Drawing, Graphics, and Photography) award at the Santa Fe Indian Art Market and is a former American Indian Graduate Center fellow. In 2009 she served as a research assistant with the Venice Biennale exhibition titled *Rendezvoused*, featuring the work of Tom Jones and Andrea Carlson. Her insights are featured in *Art in Our Lives: Native Women Artists in Dialogue* (2010). Reynolds-White Hawk's art is accessioned with the Akta Lakota Museum, the University of Wisconsin–Madison's Wisconsin Union Art Collection, and the Robert Penn Collection of Contemporary Northern Plains Indian Art of the University of South Dakota.

1 The focus of my studies has been in Native arts, thus the evidence provided here will weigh more heavily in this field and is meant to be of service to this community. Yet I sincerely hope that the analogies drawn will be of service to any individual interested in such topics, especially those involved in outsider arts.

2 In August 1999, the Ostego Institute for Native American History held the conference "Native Art History and Folk Art History: Critiquing the Paradigms," at the Fenimore Art Museum in Cooperstown, New York.

3 Cornel West, "Black Culture and Postmodernism," in *Remaking History*, Dia Art Foundation, Discussions in Contemporary Culture 4, ed. Barbara Kruger and Phil Mariani (Seattle: Bay Press, 1989), 90.

4 Colin Rhodes, *Outsider Art: Alternatives* (London: Thames and Hudson, 2000), 15.

5 The Indian Arts and Crafts Act of 1990 (Public Law 101-644) is a truth-in-advertising law that prohibits misrepresentation in marketing of Indian arts and crafts products within the United States. It is illegal to offer or display for sale, or sell any art or craft product in a manner that falsely suggests it is Indian produced, an Indian product, or the product of a particular Indian, Indian tribe, or Indian arts and crafts organization resident within the United States. For a first-time violation of the act, an individual can face civil or criminal penalties up to a $250,000 fine, a five-year prison term, or both. If a business violates the act, it can face civil penalties or can be prosecuted and fined up to $1 million. For more information on the act, visit the Department of the Interior web-

site at http://www.doi.gov/iacb/act.html.

6 Sally Anne Duncan, "Reinventing Gee's Bend Quilts in the Name of Art," in *Sacred and Profane: Voice and Vision in Southern Self-Taught Art*, ed. Carol Crown and Charles Russell (Jackson: University Press of Mississippi, 2007), 191.

7 Lucy Lippard, *Mixed Blessings: New Art in a Multicultural America* (New York: Pantheon, 1990), 6.

8 Molly H. Mullin, *Culture in the Marketplace: Gender, Art, and Value in the American Southwest* (Durham: Duke University Press, 2001), 132.

9 Gary Alan Fine, *Everyday Genius: Self-Taught Art and the Culture of Authenticity* (Chicago: University of Chicago Press, 2004), 10.

10 Karl A. Hoerig, *Under the Palace Portal: Native American Artists in Santa Fe* (Albuquerque: University of New Mexico Press, 2003), 190–91.

11 Janet C. Berlo, and Ruth B. Phillips, *Native North American Art* (Oxford: Oxford University Press, 1998), 212.

12 Julia S. Ardery, *The Temptation: Edgar Tolson and the Genesis of Twentieth-Century Folk Art* (Chapel Hill: University of North Carolina Press, 1998), 240. Ardery cites the scholarship of Suzanne Seriff.

13 Ibid., 244.

14 Ibid., 252.

15 Ibid., 229.

16 Fine, *Everyday Genius*, 43.

17 Ibid., 61.

18 Peter Selz, *Art of Engagement: Visual Politics in California and Beyond* (Los Angeles: University of California Press, 2006), 164.

19 Ibid., 165.

20 Rhodes, *Outsider Art*, 15.

21 Fine, *Everyday Genius*, 61.

22 The following is an excerpt from the Southwest Association of Indian Arts, which runs the world's largest annual Indian art market, outlining the benefits of business membership: "Santa Fe Indian Market® means big business. Hotels are filled to capacity; restaurants are booked full; car rental agencies rent every car on their lots; galleries have their busiest week of the year; and local grocery stores and department stores are filled with the artists and buyers who come to Santa Fe Indian Market®. The 80,000 visitors who come to Indian Market make it the largest attended annual event in Santa Fe. The economic impact of Santa Fe Indian Market® is estimated to be more than $100 million." See http://swaia.org/Get_Involved/Membership/index.html.

23 Mullin, *Culture in the Marketplace*, 166.

24 Hoerig, *Under the Palace Portal*, 19.

25 Charles Russell, *Self-Taught Art: The Culture and Aesthetics of American Vernacular Art* (Jackson: University Press of Mississippi, 2001), 29.

Sundays with Harry
An Essay on a Contemporary Native Artist of Our Time

Patsy Phillips

> Creating art is like my heartbeat. I need it to
> survive.
> —*Harry Fonseca*

Harry Fonseca's work is universal; his art engages world issues and in his career, he continually challenged and changed the boundaries of perception as related to Native and non-Native peoples. As a close friend and colleague of Fonseca's, I wanted to capture his thoughts about his career before his death from an inoperable brain tumor in 2006.

Throughout the last six months of his life, I called Harry on Sundays to discuss his life and art, except on those occasions when he was too sick to talk. We called it "Sundays with Harry."[1] This essay is intended as a record of those interviews, not a complete history of Fonseca's career or a history of Native arts. My narrative will raise more questions than I will be able to answer about the issues that contemporary Native artists face as historically marginalized figures in American art history and contemporary art.

While Fonseca's iconic Coyote series is widely recognized, as an artist he remains virtually unknown beyond the Native art world and has never exhibited in a major contemporary art museum. Change is

The artist Harry Fonseca with the author Patsy Phillips in his Santa Fe home, 2005. Courtesy of the author. Photograph by Mariah Sacoman.

incremental, and in this sense, my efforts here reflect the importance of advocating for the professional and artistic recognition of marginalized and excluded groups, in particular, for Native artists. Fonseca deserves to be reclassified—not categorized only as a Native artist, but also as a contemporary artist.

UNDERSTANDING COYOTE IS COMPLICATED

"Coyote paintings are complicated to analyze because they are so accessible and many people get stuck on the surface," observed the New

York contemporary artist Michael Pribich.[2] Playful and colorful images of Coyote fill Fonseca's canvases, but beneath these familiar and lively surfaces, the artist seeks to challenge popular beliefs about Native identity. Coyote figures can be urban and hip, clad in leather jackets and boots. Coyote women may sing opera, dance sensually, and sport off-the-shoulder flowered blouses.[3] Beyond these vibrant surfaces, deeper insights into Native American traditions can be found. Coyote not only entertains; he provides explanations for life and spirit on this earth. In Native American mythology, Coyote represents human contradictions such as truth and deception, joy and sadness, life and death. In life he lives by his wits and instincts, always adapting to changing times. Native peoples, like Coyote, are continuously adjusting to new ways. Living in the present but safeguarding the past, their stories will keep changing and evolving forever.

Fonseca said he "purposely placed that animal [Coyote] in a very contemporary world. I made Coyote my own . . . so naïve but wise."[4] The Coyote characters broadened the more traditional depictions of Native peoples, making their complexity and current concerns evident. By making American Indians contemporary, Fonseca expanded the public's understanding of Native peoples, their history, and their culture. In the 1990s, Fonseca's image of Coyote was everywhere in Santa Fe—on salsa jars sold at the most exclusive restaurants, on the Santa Fe Opera poster, and in event advertisements throughout the city. These reminders of Native people in the contemporary scene were accessible—both in their humorous content and in their permeation of public space. On the surface Coyote appears light and fun, but in reality it addresses the weighty issues Native peoples face today. Coyote's accessibility and attraction in turn made Native people more accessible as contemporary figures in public culture.

Fonseca remarked, "Coyote is often up against a brick wall as are so many Native peoples and artists."[5] For Fonseca, this brick wall symbolizes human frailty and vulnerability. Coyote is a personification of Fonseca's own struggles, and in an expanded sense, is representative of the challenges contemporary American Indians face: "As soon as you're born, you're up against a wall. But it's what you do when faced with obstacles that matters."[6] Native peoples are bound by generations of repression. Land appropriation, substandard housing and education, limited economic opportunities, and cultural bias are consistent factors in Indian communities. These obstacles have negatively affected the self-perception of Indian peoples for generations. This oppressive climate is apparent in the selective venues in which Native arts circulate—galleries, museums, and seasonal arts fairs with restricted categories of reception. Through Coyote, Fonseca suggests, "Freedom is the Native Americans' choice."[7] In this sense, freedom means artistic freedom to create works that challenge prevailing stereotypes as well as freedom to have that work shown in diverse arts settings.

BEYOND COYOTE

Throughout his career, Fonseca explored many different subjects and painting styles. Sitting in his studio with Jackson Pollock–like paint splattered over concrete floors, easels holding works from his different art periods, and large-scale canvases pinned to all four walls, Fonseca told Larry Abbott in a mid-1990s interview, "You look around the gallery and it looks like maybe three or four artists work here—or a crazy person— one or the other."[8] Fonseca was not locked into working with one image; instead, he continued to challenge himself. "I don't have a favorite series," stated Fonseca when he discussed his body of work.[9] In camaraderie with Coyote, Fonseca could not be backed into just one image—they were always changing. Fonseca transformed himself and his art throughout his career, but the quality and consistency of his art never wavered.

When Fonseca first started painting, he said, "there was nowhere to go with my art."[10] But he and some other California Native artists formed their own group. "We showed anywhere, including the state fair," said Fonseca.[11] "Fonseca has guided Native arts because he's been so truthful to his art," observes Gerald McMaster, curator of Canadian art at the Art Gallery of Ontario. "Unlike many artists, he was always evolving and changing."[12]

Fonseca could have capitalized on his Coyote characters throughout his whole career; however, he took chances with his work, exploring many other themes. In the late 1980s, Fonseca traveled around Utah, Arizona, and Colorado looking at rock art created by Native Americans thousands of years ago. From this research and exploration Fonseca created a series titled *Stone Poems*, based on petroglyphs of the West. In *Stone Poems*, Fonseca changed his painting technique. He no longer painted in a flat style but instead used texture on the surface, building up layers of paint and symbols, creating paintings that exploded on the canvas.

In the early 1990s, Fonseca went to Sacramento to research the history of his tribe, the Maidu. During this period, he created *Discovery of Gold and Souls in California* in response to the physical, emotional, and spiritual genocide of Native peoples. The discovery of gold led to the death of many Natives throughout California, including some of Fonseca's tribal members, at the hands of greedy prospectors and settlers. Fonseca intended to create only four pieces but later said, "I lost myself while painting the Gold series and transcended the subject matter after painting over one hundred fifteen of them."[13] In this series, Fonseca challenged the viewer to consider Native history and its consequences to Native peoples. He painted gold crosses on white backgrounds with red ochre, symbolizing Native blood, splattered over the canvases. The gold settlers' attempt to annihilate Native peoples is a part of American history that is rarely told. The Gold series transcends cultures. According to Fonseca, the crosses represent Christianity, genocide, and greed: "They are even more powerful when you think about Iraq."[14]

In the mid-1990s Fonseca began painting *St. Francis of Assisi*, an image that intrigued him for many years. St. Francis reminded Fonseca of Coyote, he said, because "St. Francis went against the tradition of the church. And he had a vision and went for it, like Coyote."[15] When he painted St. Francis, he was criticized by both Native and non-Native peoples, who asked, "Is it Indian?" Fonseca said, "Of course it is. I painted it." He painted in cycles, always returning to or including images he created, starting with Coyote. *Stone Poems, Coyote,* and *Discovery* are all represented in *St. Francis of Assisi.* In *St. Francis and Wild Ravens* (1996), Fonseca painted a blue sky peeking through a gold background with St. Francis in the center. Dotted throughout the canvas are rock art images, gold is incorporated to represent genocide and Christianity, and Coyote lives under the cloak of St. Francis as a trickster.

In 2001 Fonseca decided he no longer wanted to deal with the human spirit, so he began painting *Seasons* for spiritual inspiration.[16] In the fall, he would drive up to the Aspen groves on the side of the hills in Santa Fe to check out colors. "I learned a lot putting myself into the seasons," he said. "Autumn brought me to my knees because I was so naïve. I wanted to paint the fall during the actual season so I tried to paint in three months what it took a lifetime or more to grow. Nature is a very humbling experience."[17]

Finally, in 2004, Fonseca started what would become his final series, *Stripes,* based on the Grand Canyon landscape. He continued his interest in nature with this series. These works evolved into perfectly straight lines in brilliant colors. "Harry mastered color on the canvas. The way one color flows into the next is brilliant," declared the artist Bob Haozous.[18] *Stripes* was a continuation of the *Seasons* theme, with perfectly striped lines that mesmerize the viewer. Fonseca wanted the viewer to "get lost in the work."[19] He purposely did not suggest a theme for *Stripes,* wanting people to come up with their own interpretations. Through *Seasons* and *Stripes,* Fonseca was inviting the viewer to slow down and reflect on nature and life, as he was doing.

RAISED NATIVE

Six feet two inches tall, Fonseca had hair like Albert Einstein, full, bushy, kinky, and gray—before chemotherapy. "My hair best represents a combination of all my ethnicities. It's a mess just like me," Fonseca laughed.[20] A good-looking man, Fonseca had light mahogany skin, and his soft brown eyes smiled when he talked. Fonseca was born in 1946 in

Sacramento, California, to a Maidu/Hawaiian woman and a Portuguese man. Fonseca identified mostly with his Native family because he was raised with his mother's people; his father left the family when Fonseca was three years old. Because of this, Fonseca didn't know his father's side of the family, which he later said was one reason why he didn't paint Portuguese-themed paintings.[21] As the only artist in a family of five kids, he didn't have money to buy art paper and supplies, so Fonseca painted on the walls of his home, on cardboard, or whatever else he could find. Later he attended college, but driven by his own vision, he dropped out of Sacramento State when he felt hindered by the structure of art classes, deciding to pursue art on his own.

Fonseca credited Henri Matisse and Pablo Picasso for influencing his work the most. He appreciated Matisse's strong use of color and Picasso's viciousness of line. Jean-Michel Basquiat's exuberant liberty with color and paint also inspired Fonseca. Rick Bartow, Bob Haozous, Frank La Pena, and Jaune Quick-to-See Smith were the Native artists who influenced Fonseca's work the most. They were his good friends and artists whom he deeply respected.

In 2006, with his right hand shaky from cancer, he said, "Everything I do is directed towards my art. I have to get up. I have to paint; that's what I'm here for. It's sad in many ways because I've lost a lot of just living. The most important thing in my life, besides my daughter, Sarah, and Harry (his partner), is my artwork. It's a great love of mine. It's gotten me through so much emotionally, physically, and financially."[22] His work remained foremost in his mind; until the last month of his life, Fonseca talked about painting.

Fonseca had exhibitions in ethnographic, historical, and natural history museums, such as the Smithsonian's National Museum of the American Indian in New York City, the Institute of American Indian Arts Museum (now the Museum of Contemporary Native Arts) in Santa Fe, New Mexico, the Wheelwright Museum in Santa Fe, New Mexico, and the Oakland Museum in California. Fonseca's work has many collectors and sells for as much as $100,000 a painting. Fonseca has been lauded for his intelligence, talent, and imagination, but his work has yet to be exhibited in a major contemporary art museum. Fonseca was excluded from the contemporary art world as if he were a craftsman or an ethnographic artist who focused only on Native themes, but Fonseca was much more than a romantic Indian painter. He deserves to be considered as a contemporary artist, one who just happens to be Native.

BEYOND CULTURAL AND ETHNOGRAPHIC MUSEUMS

Native artists have long created art that is not craft-based. Native arts and cultures are dynamic, but for many non-Natives, American Indians exist in the past. For the general public, contemporary Native American is a contradiction in terms. "It's difficult to teach people that Native art has gone beyond crafts because they want to romanticize Natives and keep them in the past. People still want to see 'beads and feathers,'" suggested Kathleen Ash-Milby, curator of the Smithsonian's National Museum of the American Indian.[23]

Fonseca believed it takes more than just art to be successful. "Indian Markets are what keep us where we are today," he said.[24] What other groups primarily focus on markets to sell their work? Is race what keeps Native artists relegated to ethnographic museums? The problem, he determined, was that "artists were comfortable with their stereotypes. Takes a certain consciousness of what we've been through and going through now to change. Don't see much consciousness now. It's a threat to Indian people to let go of what we think we are."[25]

"Unfortunately, contemporary Native art is not taken seriously and has historically been neglected by art critics, art historians, and writers," suggested Truman Lowe, a studio arts professor at the University of Wisconsin, Madison, and a Ho Chunk tribal member. "It's not the Native artists' fault and it's certainly not Harry's fault. If he had gotten some reviews of his work, he would have had an impact."[26] Though influenced by and committed to his Native heritage, Fonseca did not allow this dedication to limit his artistic expression.

Fonseca could not understand why there were no serious criticisms of contemporary Native arts. He would get discouraged at the lack of interest from the contemporary art world, but he always continued to paint. "Fonseca's work represents the best of Native and European traditions, contemporary art, and his personal vision," suggested Pribich, a good friend of the artist, who had known him since he lived in Sacramento in the 1970s. "Harry's mix of influences is the best of America in that he consumed so much of culture and life, and he gave it back," he added. "America is unique in that a person can move beyond boundaries to accomplish something new—Fonseca moved a lot of barriers, yet few outside Native arts know him. It's a shame."[27]

The contemporary artist John Baldassari suggested that the real problem for Fonseca was not his art per se, but rather his location—that he lived in Santa Fe, New Mexico. "Santa Fe is a niche market and as long as he lives there, he will not be recognized as a serious artist," Baldassari said.[28] However, several famous contemporary artists such as Agnes Martin and Georgia O'Keeffe had their beginnings in Santa Fe, and Bruce Nauman lives in the area. Santa Fe is considered the third most important art market in the United States, after New York and Los Angeles. Major contemporary art exhibitions are shown at SITE Santa Fe and art galleries throughout town. And the Museum of Contemporary Native Arts is showing progressive contemporary exhibitions. So why aren't Native artists who live in Santa Fe taken seriously as contemporary artists? Do Native artists have to move away from Santa Fe to be appreciated? Why would there be different standards for Native artists? Does it really matter? "There's a certain kind of perspective that's hard to move out of in the Southwest," observed Lowe.[29]

FINAL DIAGNOSIS

"The hardest part of this cancer is losing my independence and not being able to paint," Fonseca said five months after the cancer diagnosis. Bedridden and the right hand he once painted with now paralyzed, Fonseca continued to paint with his words: "When I paint again, I will remake Coyote once more."[30] Fonseca wanted Coyote to personify where Natives are today. "I would like to really spiff him up from when I first started," he said. "We finally have Native doctors and lawyers, and the National Museum of the American Indian."[31] Fonseca expressed his wish to paint Coyote wearing a pink shirt, purple tie, pinstriped suit, and wingtip shoes, and carrying a briefcase. Maybe he'll go to Washington, D.C., next: "I'd like to see what kind of brick wall he comes up against today."[32] At the time of Harry's final illness, the Acoma poet Simon Ortiz once again referenced the coyote in a memorial poem:

> Harry, I understand, Coyote brother, the how and why and why not
> Coyote needs to laugh—so we can love those who make us feel
> contradictions we need to see, that we need to realize, that we
> need to know what our lives have become! To see, to know.
>
> Harry, thank you for making me and others feel welcome to see
> the contradictions you and Coyote see and show us, especially now.[33]

In Fonseca's lifetime, he witnessed contemporary Native arts advance from a small group in California exhibiting at state fairs to a national museum dedicated solely to Native arts and cultures. In anticipation of the Smithsonian's National Museum of the American Indian (NMAI) grand opening in Washington, D.C., in 2004, Fonseca began painting the *Maidu Creation Story* on a large scale. He first told me about it in 2002 when I was working for the NMAI. As an insider, I knew the museum wasn't collecting new works if they weren't directly related to the inaugural exhibitions. Fonseca wasn't discouraged by the lack of funds and kept working toward his vision. Completing the work in 2005, a serious collector of Fonseca's paintings purchased the *Maidu Creation Story* for $100,000 and donated it to the NMAI. In early spring 2006, the year of his death, Fonseca visited the National Museum of the American Indian to see the work, where it still hangs today on the third floor.

Harry Fonseca's heart stopped beating on December 28, 2006, six months after he was diagnosed with an inoperable brain tumor. At the time of his death, he was surrounded by friends, art collectors, and family, including his longtime partner, Harry Nungessor. This memorial essay is dedicated to Harry Fonseca's life and art.

AUTHOR BIOGRAPHY

Patsy Phillips, an enrolled Cherokee, is the director of the Museum of Contemporary Native Arts, based in Santa Fe, New Mexico. Before joining MoCNA, Phillips worked at the Smithsonian's National Museum of the American Indian as a development officer and director of special projects. Phillips holds a master's degree in writing from the Johns Hopkins University, a graduate certificate in museum studies from Harvard University, and a bachelor's degree in anthropology from Southern Methodist University.

NOTES

1   Telephone interviews with Harry Fonseca, June–December, 2006. Harry and I were close friends. I first met him when I was invited by Dr. Nancy Marie Mithlo to work on an exhibit for the Venice Biennale in 1996. We met monthly for well over a year planning this exhibition. In 1999 a small group of individuals traveled to Venice for the Biennale, including myself, Harry, and Dr. Mithlo. I fell in love with Harry on this trip, and he remained a kind, loving, and thoughtful friend until his death in December 2006.

2   Michael Pribich, in conversation with the author, July 2007, New York, New York.

3   For illustrations of Fonseca's work, see his official Web site, http://www.harryfonseca.com.

4   Fonseca, November 2006.

5   Fonseca, August 2006.

6   Ibid.

7   Ibid.

8   Larry Abbott, "Harry Fonseca: A Time of Visions." See http://www.britesites.com/native_artist_interviews.

9   Fonseca, October 2006.

10   Fonseca, November 2006.

11   Ibid.

12   Gerald McMaster, in conversation with the author, June 2006, Santa Fe, New Mexico.

13   Fonseca, October 2006.

14   Ibid.

15   Ibid.

16   Fonseca, November 2006.

17   Ibid.

18   Bob Haozous, in conversation with the author, December 8, 2006, Santa Fe, New Mexico.

19   Fonseca, October 2006.

20   Fonseca, November 2006.

21   Fonseca, October 2006.

22   Fonseca, August 2006.

23   Kathleen Ash-Milby, in conversation with the author, August 2007, New York, New York.

24   Fonseca, September 2006.

25   Ibid.

26 Truman Lowe, in conversation
with the author, June 2007,
Venice, Italy.

27 Pribich, July 2007.

28 John Baldassari, in conversation
with the author, December 2006.

29 Lowe, November 2006.

30 Fonseca, November 2006.

31 Ibid.

32 Ibid.

33 See http://www.harryfonseca.
com/news/index.htm.

Reading Beneath the Surface
Joe Feddersen's Parking Lot

heather ahtone

INDIGENOUS AESTHETIC

Every time an Indigenous artist creates an object that reflects concepts rooted within her culture, this same artist is perpetuating that culture one more day as an act of self-determination. This is done every day, as artists across the continent participate in the creative process that has served as a cornerstone within Indigenous cultural communities. While every effort of political and religious assault has been made historically to subdue these same cultures, their survival can be partially attributed to the continued production of visual and performance arts. As long as Indigenous people continue to use the arts to reflect unique experiences within a contemporary society, they are fundamentally breathing life into these cultures. Because the vitality of these cultures is so closely tied to the creative process, it is important, therefore, that work by Indigenous artists be considered within a framework that incorporates Indigenous epistemology. Analyzing the arts from a cultural perspective will reinforce these acts of self-determination, both bolstering how we understand these individual artistic expressions and expanding our capacity to understand and share this Indigeneity.

The methodology employed here is based on research involving the analysis of cultural materials, including how these materials were constructed, the traditions involved therein, and their function within a traditional Indigenous community. What I hope to offer is an example

of the value of applying an Indigenous-based methodology as a basis
for interdisciplinary research. Ideas about what might constitute an
Indigenous aesthetic are still in their infant stages of development, and
should not be assumed to reflect a comprehensive or thoroughly vetted
methodology. There are flaws, as there will be with this kind of exploration. But the need to develop a framework that centers on Indigenous
cultural values and beliefs bolsters my courage, and so I offer my ideas
here for consideration.

In order to develop a language addressing this cultural perspective, one must acknowledge that Indigenous epistemology does not
coalesce with Western epistemology. Perhaps this is self-evident, but
it must be stated in order to allow for the discussion that just as they do
not coalesce, nor do they run parallel or perpendicular. This distinction between "ways of knowing" is important, as it allows that bodies
of knowledge reflect the cultural values and beliefs on which they are
grounded—there does not exist a universal measure. Thus one cannot imagine an Indigenous aesthetic while using Western cultural standards. If we allow that this shift from a Western to an Indigenous paradigm is possible, then we must look to the cultural source in seeking
a foundation.

The framework needed to analyze an Indigenous aesthetic must
come from within the cultures themselves. Each tribal culture has local
ideals, values, and beliefs that necessarily require consideration. These
can be incorporated into a larger framework that allows for discussion of
the art in a broader continental manner, which I assert can be useful in
understanding the Indigenous aesthetic. Through careful consideration
of an object's materiality, the artist's use of metaphor and symbolism,
and the role of cultural reciprocity, it can be placed within a context that
will lend a fuller understanding of the object as contemporary art.

JOE FEDDERSEN'S *PARKING LOT*

This essay will focus on *Parking Lot* by Joe Feddersen (b. 1953, Colville
Confederated Tribes) to explore how this methodology can reveal the
cultural context of an object that might otherwise be unavailable. In
Feddersen's case, it is relevant to consider an author who has proven in-
sightful and intuitive in his approach to contemporary Indigenous art.
Jackson Rushing delivers a sensitive review of Joe Feddersen's *Plateau
Geometrics* in his essay "Sacred Geometry," writing:

> The "Plateau Geometric" prints are "open" and accessible
> to a modernist reading based on formalism and the linear
> logic of "advanced" art. But contained within them are
> kinds of knowledge—personal and tribal—that are no
> less codified but are based on poetic responses to living

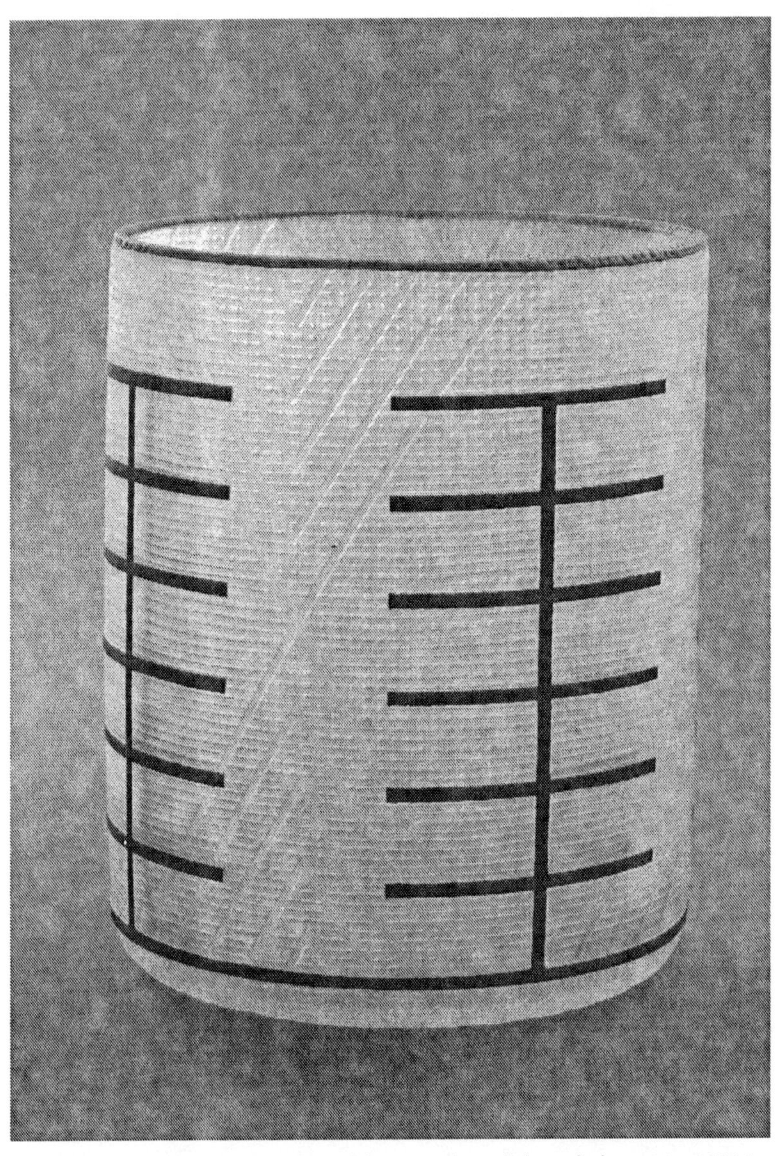

Joe Feddersen, *Parking Lot,* 2003, blown and sandblasted glass, 14 x 10¾ in. (35.56 x 27.30 cm.), Collection of the Nerman Museum of Contemporary Art, Johnson County Community College, Overland Park, Kansas. Courtesy of the artist. Photograph by Bill Bachhuber.

in a particular place. Access to this information is, if not "closed," then certainly experientially restricted. By way of his homesickness, Feddersen gives a glimpse of that knowledge. But because that glimpse takes the form of discrete symbols derived from stylized patterns that are historically and culturally constructed, we must accept that a vast space lies between "here" and "there."[1]

I quote Rushing because he is expressing an honest recognition that more is present in Feddersen's work than is accessible through a Western art historical approach. Rushing's acknowledgment of this allows me to offer a bridge to traverse the "vast space" that exists between a Western and Indigenous approach to the object.

The "here" lies in the tangible presence of *Parking Lot*. This glass form is from the *Urban Indian* series (2003 onward), when printmaker Joe Feddersen began working with glass artist Preston Singletary to create a new body of work to be exhibited at the NMAI. These three-dimensional forms were a culmination of several ideas coming together for Feddersen through a new medium. Within this work, Feddersen integrated references to the Okanagan basket forms he had woven since the mid-1990s, the traditional symbols found in his tribe's Plateau-based cultural materials, and the signs that marked his two-dimensional print work.

The milky white glass of *Parking Lot* is presented in a wide cylinder form, referring to a wide-mouthed Plateau-style storage basket called a "sally bag" (14 x 10¾ in.). With three layers of textures on its exterior surface, the form carries a juxtaposition of symbols. The under layer of glass is etched with a contrapuntal chevron design that repeats four times around the exterior of the form. Over the entire surface is a shallower etched grid of irregular tiny squares that reference the warp and weft texture of a twined basket. On the surface, in each of the four voids between the chevron designs, is laid a diagram with four vertically oriented linear arrangements—the eponymous parking lot. The interior of the vessel is smooth and has a contrasting glassy sheen to the matted exterior. The rim of the vessel has an olive green band. The base is slightly rounded along the exterior edge, referencing the curve of a handwoven basket. The scale of the vessel is relative to a gathering basket, large enough to carry a bushel of fruit. *Parking Lot* is striking with the gentle glow of the etched white glass underneath the simplicity of the black lines.

MATERIALITY

In order to fully appreciate the elements that Feddersen has incorporated into *Parking Lot* and how they reflect an Indigenous aesthetic, I have paid attention to the object's materiality—a term used here to describe how materials and designs serve as extensions of the Indigenous traditions.[2] The Okanagan people are part of the Colville Confederated Tribes, whose lands are located in Washington State, where Feddersen was born. The Okanagan people are also recognized in the Canadian province of British Columbia, where Feddersen's mother was born. Located in the intermountain western area of the Plateau region, Feddersen's tribe speaks the Okanagan language, which is part of the Salish language family. Unique linguistic affiliations and design elements thus relate to many of the tribes that have occupied the region between the Columbia River and the Pacific Northwest coast since time immemorial.

The geographic location of the Okanagan people in Washington State also implicates the sharing of ideas, designs, and forms with other tribes of the Plateau area and the Northern Plains, via an expansive trade system that existed in the region. The Okanagan are situated within one of the most important trade centers in western North America at the confluence of the Columbia, Fraser, and Dalles River systems. The interactive range of this trade system was instrumental in connecting people from the upper West Coast with the Northern Plains cultures and beyond. These multiple influences have imposed limitations for scholarship in that the provenance of specific forms and designs is difficult to ascertain. As Gaylord Torrence points out in his analysis of the parfleches materials from this region, designs become difficult to attribute to a particular tribe: "Parfleches were freely traded throughout the region, to the extent that all types were almost equally dispersed among all the tribes by the time substantial collecting had begun. With this trade occurred the continuous exchange of design concepts, so that any design developed by one group was very likely to have been appropriated by others."[3] Since baskets were used in the trade commerce of the region, it is logical to expect that baskets and related designs were likewise shared and appropriated. But Torrence has based his comments on catalog information largely available through museum and private collections, though these sources are known to be woefully superficial in their documentation of historically collected materials.[4] I offer that local tribal artists, such as Feddersen, can be considered valuable resources for information about how the designs and materials were and continue to be used, especially as these traditions persist into present-day cultural production.

Along this vein of reasoning, *Parking Lot* is similar in form to other known Plateau baskets. In all three essays in Feddersen's mid-career retrospective exhibition catalog, *Vital Signs*, the authors reference the form of a "sally bag"[5] as an inspiration for Feddersen's own weaving work and as a formal reference in the shapes of the glass vessels. Within a Plateau cultural premise, women would use these bags specifically as gathering baskets. A brief comparison between the glass vessels and the basketry reflects the three-dimensional reading as similar, but there is a difference in the proportion and scale. Sally bags are commonly smaller in height and narrower with softened sides.[6] The sally bag forms do not have the wide, open mouth, and substantive structure seen in glass form of *Parking Lot*. When asked about this difference in the structure of the baskets, Feddersen said, "Part of that is that I was working with somebody, and trying to have a glass form makes it more difficult, because it goes against everything that the glass wants to do. I was working with Preston and he can make beautiful cylinder forms because the glass wants to do that and it's hard for him not to do that. . . . And it's also about referencing and mimicking. Sometimes you use the basket as a departure point in creating something, but I don't think I have to mimic it."[7] The reference to mimicking explains the autonomy that Feddersen exercises in using the traditional designs and forms within his art. This autonomy makes the glass vessel more complex to interpret formally, because it is difficult to gauge what is a direct act of cultural mimesis and what is artistic innovation. For this reason, Feddersen's cooperation has been instrumental in the research for this essay.

The glass cannot be dismissed as simply an exploration on the artist's part into new materials. Feddersen's knowledge of basket making and previous work in installation could certainly have been used to create the spatial expanse he was seeking for the gallery at the NMAI. Additionally, glass is not limited in color or scale, as exemplified in the work of Singletary. The choice to use milky white glass has to be considered more closely. Elizabeth Woody, who described Feddersen's work for the *Continuum 12* exhibition catalog, wrote, "Feddersen's use of glass speaks of our human fragility."[8] One can also see the glass as a delicate metaphor for the relationship that people have to their cultural materials. The rapid decline of traditional art forms over the last hundred years for many tribes has had a significant impact on the process of passing traditional knowledge on from one generation to another. Using a traditional form in concert with the glass, the color white can be seen as Woody describes, "the shell of the basket with the ephemeral density of a cloud."[9] Perhaps the white glass can also be seen as a transformation of the wax paper Feddersen used in his previous experiments with basket forms, which like glass is altered by the hand and heat. The range of interpretations Feddersen allows in the materiality, through the tribally specific use and reference to materials, is repeated in his direct invocation of design symbols.

METAPHOR/SYMBOLISM

Feddersen's use of signs and symbols has been part of his stylistic exploration as an artist. In 2001 he produced a series called *Plateau Geometrics* that included printmaking and basketry, all incorporating layers of abstractions, both Indigenous and Euro-American. Describing his motivation to develop this body of work, Feddersen said, "I decided I wanted to do work about home, about the Plateau area, because I was really intrigued by how much we use abstract designs. A lot of my early work on the *Plateau Geometrics* series was based on that kind of situation and also being a printmaker. I wanted to celebrate both of those, the designs and the medium and at the same time; I wanted to celebrate where I was from. I didn't want it to be didactic or anything, I just wanted to align the forms and color, formally."[10] Feddersen's expressed interest in creating a dialogue between the abstract Indigenous cultural designs and non-Indigenous materials, begun in the medium of printmaking, created the impetus for his later work in glass. Within printmaking, Feddersen worked with the ideas that later developed into the *Urban Indian* series.[11]

Using the sally bag form and tradition as guides, Feddersen provided for the interpretation of symbols on the surface of the glass vessel.[12] In *Parking Lot,* Feddersen offers critical information necessary for reading the chevron design etched into the surface. He said, "When you're looking at the chevron design, those are actually the designs for *woman* in Plateau culture, kind of like an hourglass design, kind of a winding vase."[13] The symbolic reference to woman is directly drawn from his local community. Feddersen has described learning from Okanagan basket makers the designs and materials related to this artistic tradition:

> I did spend a weekend talking with one of our tribal elders.
> She's known for her baskets and I spent a day talking with
> her. I wanted to learn about the designs and all of the reeds
> and their relationship and we talked. . . . And then she does
> this really wonderful thing where she said at the end of
> the day this design means this but in the next valley over
> it means something totally different. So this whole thing
> about the culture and the context is also kind of idiosyn-
> cratic depending on where you're from. The interpretation
> can be different from just a few miles away.[14]

The idiosyncratic nature of Indigenous designs and symbols puts a responsibility on the artist and art historian to consider these as semiotic references in context with their meanings. In this case, when Feddersen uses the symbol for woman, he invigorates it as a continued part of the cultural dialogue and, by doing so, also contemporizes the language in its usage.

Further, by placing the symbol of woman on this form, Feddersen calls into play the concept of woman as the Okanagan people understand it. With this translation of the symbol defined by Feddersen, it cannot be ignored that within Okanagan culture, as part of the larger community of Colville traditions, woman is a living metaphor for the earth. While some may consider this a chauvinistic construct to be used by this male artist, it is necessary to see that aligning the concept of woman with the earth is not held here within the Western dynamic of "woman as nature," with the subtext that both are to be dominated by men. Rather, one must look with the eyes of an Okanagan person, for whom the earth is described as a woman "who gives birth to life forms."[15] If we look to the genesis story for the Colville, it becomes more evident how woman is a symbolic description of the relationship that these people have with the earth: "Old-One, or Chief, made the earth out of a woman, and said she would be the mother of all the people. Thus the earth was once a human being, and she is alive yet; but she has been transformed, and we cannot see her in the same way we can see a person. Nevertheless she has legs, arms, head, heart, flesh, bones, and blood. The soil is her flesh; the trees and vegetation are her hair; the rocks, her bones; and the wind is her breath. She lies spread out, and we live upon her."[16]

The familial affection that many Indigenous community members have for the earth is far deeper than can be examined from a Western perspective, which largely sees the earth as a form of property. Seeing the earth as a woman who is the source for nurturing and creation extends beyond the feminine object and into a broader relationship, which Dennis Martinez has recently coined as "kincentricity."[17] Martinez uses this term to describe the circular interaction between humans and the earth, which makes their relationship more closely guided by principles evident in nature seeking a harmonious balance. For the Colville people, as with many communities, the creative force of woman is evident not only in the role of the human mother but also in the earth's capacity to provide and nurture all that lives on her surface. Feddersen's use of this hourglass symbol is not just an aesthetic design choice, but the invocation of deep emotional and cultural ties to womanhood and all this represents. Feddersen has also symbolically layered the subtle texture of a basket weave on the surface of the glass. By doing so, he draws the reference between the natural weaving materials of grass, seen symbolically as the hair of the earth, and the glass, thereby aligning the delicate nature of the glass to the delicate relationship between Indigenous people and their homelands.

Etching this highly charged symbol for earth below a parking lot design then merits attention to the practical and metaphorical reading of their combination. The parking lot design, really a diagram, was developed in the late 1920s to allow for the development of large department stores and facilitated the advent of the automobile culture.[18] These diagrams can be seen to represent the daily migration patterns of contemporary society—driving to work, to the grocery store, to school, and so forth. Migrating within these terms also requires that we consider that this is done largely on asphalt- or cement-finished roads. Organizing patterns of migration, here represented by a parking lot diagram, form the basis of how most Americans relate to the earth— through a mediated system of transit routes, either roads or sidewalks that "improve" the surface to become more suitable for human use. The roads and sidewalks become a way of marking where humans are encouraged to travel, to move over the surface of the earth, which in

Colville cultural beliefs is mother of us all. The simplicity of the glass surface comes to be seen as revealing a very antithetical relationship between the people and their mother. This juxtaposition of symbols also draws into relationship the two designs as markers of place and belonging, here revealing a contrast between Indigenous and Euro-American ideals of relating to the earth.

The interplay of culture, through layers of visibility, might also read as a metaphorical rendering of the Indigenous experience. Feddersen achieves a subtle tension because of the shared relationship the designs have as simplified geometric symbols. Also, the form of *Parking Lot* as a vessel is closely tied to Feddersen's western Plateau baskets. Through his syncretistic use of abstract designs on this vessel, Feddersen reveals an Indigenous aesthetic emphasis on symbolism and metaphor as a codified subtext to the visually appealing layers.

RECIPROCITY

An emphasis on symbolism and metaphor is intrinsic to the role of reciprocity within Indigenous art. Reciprocity is largely an act of gratitude by an artist for their cultural heritage. By using traditional art forms and designs, artists are actively participating in the continuation of their cultures. Feddersen recognizes this role and sees the need and the potential for evolving the Okanagan traditional forms and designs to reflect a contemporary Indigenous experience. He describes it as follows:

> A lot of times our signs are from our surroundings and our landscape. I've always been cognizant of how place is related to the culture. To think about people from the Plateau area going out and recording the landscape for thousands of years and having this relationship is like a coming of age. This tie with the land goes beyond the hundreds or thousands of years of people going out into the land and the way that the land was forming the culture. I think that's really important also. I think part of that is embedded in the visual culture. It's not a singular kind of thing. It was repeated for centuries. We've been in our present place for over a hundred years now. Everyday we see the railroad tracks and we've incorporated that into our traditional designs. I've incorporated the electric lines that got put up in the '20s and '30s. It's not like what I'm doing is anything new, it's just carrying on a tradition.[19]

Feddersen uses the term "vital signs" to describe this incorporation of signs into his contemporary visual vocabulary. The term is most often associated with the measurable bodily pulses that signify human life.

In reference to his work, "vital signs" is used to reference the cultural designs, signs, and symbols that have been used within his tribal culture as a contemporary recording of their experience for millennia. He intends the ambiguity of this term, saying, "We think that to carry on the traditions, the mere act of using them enlivens them as active rather than not using them. By using the traditional signs we talk about what the meaning is and they become part of our visual vocabulary rather than something that is purely historical."[20] It would seem, then, that "vital signs" signifies the pulse of the culture as it is represented by the designs.

The act of using Indigenous designs is a form of cultural reciprocity, participating in a cycle of accountability that contributes toward the perseverance of traditional culture. When Indigenous people actively practice, participate, and perpetuate their cultures, this is the most basic form of gratitude to those ancestors who made the effort to carry the culture into the future, into our present.

CONCLUSION

It is necessary to pursue this kind of cultural and artistic analysis in order to realize the fullest value that the work offers. These references of shape and subtly etched design elements mark it as an extension of the traditions of Plateau baskets and Okanagan culture. Through their applications in a contemporary and nontraditional medium, they refute the historicized context within which Indigenous art is so often placed. It is this invocation of the past into the present that reflects an Indigenous concept of circular time, the importance of cycles and repetition as a conduit to cultural persistence.

Feddersen sees the greater advantage of working toward making traditional values vital in the contemporary world. This is succinctly described by artist–writer Gail Tremblay in *Vital Signs*: "For this series, Feddersen used his new abstract visual language to express the importance of honoring traditional patterns of culture and maintaining its vitality; at the same time, he refused to allow his artwork to lock American Indian people in some strange ethnographic present where they must not be modern if they are to be authentically 'Indian.' In these works, Feddersen makes both tradition and modernity present in contemporary American art and reflects the real lives of people living in twenty-first-century urban Indian culture."[21] By examining *Parking Lot* through a methodology that addresses the cultural context for its materiality, the artist's use of metaphors and symbols, and how contemporary Indigenous art acts as a form of reciprocity, we arrive at the "there" that Rushing could see but not reach. We are reaching an understanding of the Indigenous aesthetic.

Indigenous people must also exert effort to consider, examine, analyze, and, most important, think constructively about our Indigenous aesthetic as part of the efforts to survive and thrive. As I have done with *Parking Lot*, others are doing with Indigenous languages and literature. Through a process that seeks its foundation within the culture, we gain greater understanding of how the Indigenous epistemology informs our contemporary experience. This process reveals how Indigenous aesthetics are as much about the beauty of the object as they are about the value of beauty.

AUTHOR BIOGRAPHY

heather ahtone has curated contemporary art exhibits, taught Native science and art history, and researched the evolution of tribal design usage and materials. She is developing an interdisciplinary approach to analyzing Indigenous art, especially tribes' place-based knowledge of the environment and how this is represented in their cosmology and designs. She is committed to supporting the larger Oklahoma tribal community and especially her tribal communities, the Chickasaw and Choctaw Nations. She is Curator of Native American and Non-Western Art at the Fred Jones Jr. Museum of Art at the University of Oklahoma.

NOTES

This article was originally a paper given on February 9, 2011, as a part of the College Art Association's 99th Annual Conference panel session titled "Toward an Indigenous Artistic Sovereignty: Theorizing Contemporary Native Art," chaired by Dylan A. T. Miner, at Michigan State University.

1 W. Jackson Rushing, "Joe Feddersen: Sacred Geometry," in *After the Storm: The Eiteljorg Fellowship for Native American Fine Art, 2001*, ed. W. Jackson Rushing (Seattle: Eiteljorg Museum of American Indians and Western Art, in association with the University of Washington Press, 2001), 39.

2 Materiality as employed here is referring to how the materials implicate a specific cultural practice that is important—that which is not merely of form but of substance, as might be used in reference to legal materiality.

3 Gaylord Torrence, *The American Indian Parfleche: A Tradition of Abstract Painting* (Seattle: University of Washington Press, 1994), 229.

4 Five years of Native American object research for exhibition development has taught me that museum collections rarely have more than a tribal attribution, seldom identifying a maker or the cultural context of the object.

5 According to the University of Washington Burke Museum's online guide to Northwest coast basketry, "Although there are numerous interpretations explaining the origin of this name, there is not one definitive explanation." See http://www.washington.edu/burkemuseum/baskets/Teachersguideforbasketry.htm.

6 There is a broad variety of forms referred to as sally bags within museum collection records found

in the area. Most identified as sally bags are smaller, freestanding with twined exteriors, and lined on the interior with cloth.

7 Joe Feddersen, in conversation with the author, March 12, 2010.

8 Elizabeth Woody, "Joe Feddersen: Geometric Abstraction—the Language of the Land," in *Continuum 12* (New York: National Museum of the American Indian, 2003), 3.

9 Ibid.

10 Joe Feddersen, in conversation with the author, March 12, 2010.

11 Rushing, "Joe Feddersen: Sacred Geometry."

12 The difficulties of establishing an Indigenous cultural provenance for the form also apply to the designs. For this reason, this analysis will limit any specific reading of Indigenous designs to the western Plateau area, except for those that Feddersen identifies as belonging to his community specifically. It may require intensive local research with the Okanagan people to establish the designs as distinctive to a particular tribe or subgroup. For the purposes of this analysis, conversations with Feddersen have been instrumental in clarifying details in relation to *Parking Lot.*

13 Feddersen, in conversation with the author, March 12, 2010.

14 Ibid.

15 John A. Grim, "Cosmogony and the Winter Dance: Native American Ethics in Transition," *Journal of Religious Ethic* 20, no. 2 (1992): 389.

16 Susan Staiger Gooding, "Interior Salishan Creation Stories: Historical Ethics in the Making," *Journal of Religious Ethics* 20, no. 2 (1992): 357.

17 D. Martinez (interviewee) and D. E. Hall (interviewer), "Native Perspectives on Sustainability: Dennis Martinez (O'odham/ Chicano/Anglo)," 2008 interview transcript. See the Native Perspectives on Sustainability project Web site, http://www .nativeperspectives.net.

18 John A. Jakle and Keith A. Sculle, *Lots of Parking: Land Use in a Car Culture* (Charlottesville: University of Virginia Press, 2004).

19 Joe Feddersen in conversation with the author, March 12, 2010.

20 Ibid.

21 Gail Tremblay, "Speaking in a Language of Vital Signs," in Rebecca J. Dobkins, *Joe Feddersen: Vital Signs* (Seattle: Hallie Ford Museum of Art, Willamette University, in association with the University of Washington Press, 2008), 48.

American Indian Art
Teaching and Learning

Melanie Anne Herzog and Sarah Anne Stolte

INTRODUCTION:
AMERICAN INDIAN ART HISTORY

American Indian art history is recognized today as a field of study, but very few colleges or universities currently offer courses in American Indian—or Native American—art.[1] This essay will consider several approaches to teaching American Indian art, such as American Indian art survey courses (and Native artists' engagement with modernism as vital to these surveys); "world art" courses that focus on indigenous arts; and courses that position American Indian art, including contemporary Native art, as integral to the history of art in North America. The emphases of these courses will vary, but any of these approaches to Native American art history necessitates a reconceptualization of art history's discursive frameworks, canonical narratives, and assumptions about art, artists, and representation. Critical engagement with indigenous methods and knowledge is crucial to this reframing, and must be foregrounded as key course content.

While contemporary Native American art and art history tend to operate in what W. Jackson Rushing has termed "the fertile interstitial zone that critical theory and cultural studies have created between art history and anthropology," the production, reception, and study of Native art has historically been laden with deeply problematic assumptions about art, artists, and indigenous cultures.[2] The discourse of

Native American art history is generally understood to have begun in the second half of the nineteenth century, when anthropologists, photographers, explorers, and others eagerly collected American Indian art and artifacts.[3] To these predominantly European American collectors, the material culture of the indigenous peoples of the Americas represented evidence of a "dying" culture. Objects were hoarded as "oddities" and "curiosities" in private collections and in those of larger institutions that were established during this period, such as the Smithsonian Institution and the American Museum of Natural History. In the late nineteenth century, non-Native photographers documented what they presumed to be vanishing indigenous life, and anthropologists amassed great collections of various objects with the same intentions. These objects, many still on display in museums, were created by members of cultures that continue to thrive despite the threat of extinction. The creation of these institutions, intended to house these kinds of artifacts and historical objects, established the study of Native American art through exhibitions of material culture, most often interpreted through an anthropological lens that presumes the embodiment within these objects of a "tradition" that is static, ahistorical, and on the verge of extinction.

Private collectors, traders, and popular writers also contributed to the early study of Native American art. Beginning in the latter part of the nineteenth century, deliberate marketing strategies affected Native art production, technique, style, and iconography.[4] The desire for "authentic" Native expressions drove the collecting by non-Native tourists and ethnographers in the Southwest of pottery, baskets, Navajo weavings, and drawings and watercolor paintings. The Arts and Crafts movement's valorization of California baskets as manifestations of a fantasized era of natural domesticity, peaceful coexistence with the Spanish settlers, and harmony with the land also contributed to European Americans' appreciation of Native American material culture—prompting a shift from an "artifact" to a "souvenir" to a "work of art" paradigm.[5] Because the demands of the dominant culture determined which works of art were understood as "authentic" and "traditional"—which in turn shaped their consumption in the marketplace—indigenous agency regarding Native works of art, as well as other aspects of Native people's lives, was generally ignored. For example, the life and work of the Washoe basket maker Louisa Keyser (ca. 1835–1925) was mythologized by her patrons Abe and Amy Cohn, while Keyser's own voice was noticeably absent from the narrative they created, resulting in distortion of the historical record of this time.[6] In general, the absence of Native perspectives in publications on these baskets, and the lack of documentation of Native responses to the fascination baskets held for non-Native collectors, prevailed at the turn of the last century and beyond. In contrast, more contemporary resources, such as the National Museum of the American Indian's online exhibition *The Language of Native American*

Baskets, which features the perspectives of Native basket makers, counter these omissions.[7]

Perceptions of Native art began to shift in the mid-twentieth century. In 1941 the exhibition *Indian Art of the United States* at the Museum of Modern Art in New York displayed American Indian artwork together with European American "fine arts." Although judged through the eyes of the dominant culture, indigenous works were beginning to be appreciated in aesthetic terms. But still, Native arts were mostly valued for their influence on European American artistic modernism, and indigenous perspectives regarding the exhibited works of art continued to be absent. Fortunately, this attitude is changing—witness the "fertile interstitial zone" to which Rushing refers; still, the Native arts that continue to garner the most art historical attention are too often those that either predate the past one hundred years or those that appear strongly rooted in "traditional" art practices, rather than arts that engage contemporary practices, materials, and issues. The Cherokee scholar John Haworth, director of the National Museum of the American Indian's George Gustav Heye Center in New York, writes, "We recognize that Native artists have far too frequently been marginalized or ignored by the mainstream art world of curators, collectors, and critics. Historic objects made by Indians command top dollar at art auctions. And many 'Indian markets' give substantial attention to tradition-based textiles, ceramics, basketry, and beadwork made by living Native people. Considerably less attention is paid to contemporary Native 'gallery' art—paintings, sculpture, public art, installations, performance art, multimedia art, and conceptually based and site-specific pieces that reflect contemporary techniques and aesthetics or comment on today's issues."[8] Similarly, the Cherokee artist Kay WalkingStick calls for greater attention to contemporary art: "Good, risky, original art is being done by Native Americans, and it is this work that must be shown and supported by serious galleries and museums. This art has been developed by individuals educated in the traditions of twentieth-century modernism, but also in touch with their Indian heritage, their cultural differences, and their spiritual concerns. It is deserving of serious critical analysis and it takes no great leap of faith to analyze or appreciate it."[9]

In teaching Native American art, perspective matters. Students need to grapple with the political, spiritual, social, and economic effects of colonialism for indigenous peoples—and the discursive resonance of colonialism across academic disciplines, including art history—and they need to understand how postcolonial discourse might reverberate within these material and intellectual contexts. As well, students must become aware of ways in which colonial and postcolonial narratives inform the production of knowledge about Native and non-Native art, including how art has been studied, written about, and exhibited. All of this necessitates students' examination of the assumptions they bring to the study of Native art. It is our task as educators to facilitate students' exploration of new ways of thinking about art, and to help them learn to interrogate the historical exigencies and theoretical bases of these perspectives. Whether Native or non-Native, as educators we all need to center Native perspectives in our teaching as we design and instruct courses that look at the interconnections in Native art among aesthetics, materials, function, meaning, social relations, and social practices, and the historical circumstances within which these works of art are produced.

AMERICAN INDIAN
ART SURVEY COURSES

Courses that survey Native American and First Nations art from various regions are generally designed to first consider pre-contact indigenous arts and then address the changes that came about with the arrival of Europeans to this continent. With a focus on post-contact Native American art, these surveys give particular attention to the effects of encounters between Indian and non-Indian peoples, and to art produced under the duress of dislocation, genocide, and U.S. government policies of assimilation. Some American Indian Art survey courses incorporate twentieth- and twenty-first-century Native art into this sort of regional investigation, while others explore art of the past one hundred years, with a focus on the circumstances of its production and the intersections of Indian and non-Indian arts and cultures.

The art historical narratives constructed and enacted in teaching about Native art shape students' understanding not only of American Indian art but of art history as a discursive field as well. In their introduction to *Native North American Art*, Janet Catherine Berlo and Ruth B. Phillips remind us that "the survey, like all forms of narrative, shapes the story it tells."[10] Like most surveys, theirs is for the most part chronological, although they emphasize in the introduction that "Aboriginal conceptions of time are often organized around principles of cyclical rather than linear order."[11] Thus subsequent chapters of their survey, each devoted to a region of Native North America, incorporate examples of contemporary art that are linked conceptually to the historic arts of these regions. In addition, Berlo and Phillips problematize the typical non-Native division of Native American history into two periods, pre- and post-European contact, as this division foregrounds the availability of written texts as post-contact historical records in contrast to the archeological materials that generally serve as a primary source of study of pre-contact visual culture. This divide also suggests a period of cultural stasis that denies the dynamics of intercultural contact and exchange that preceded the arrival of Europeans to this continent.

Though their survey begins much earlier, Berlo and Phillips's historical narrative is predominantly a story of five hundred years of "suc-

cessive visual responses to crises such as epidemics, forced removals
from homelands, repressive colonial regimes, religious conversion, and
contact with foreign cultures and their arts."[12] However, the responses
of Native artists have not only been reactions to the catastrophe of colonization but are also acts of negotiation, adaptation, and resistance—
what the Anishinaabe writer and literary theorist Gerald Vizenor has
termed "survivance." Survivance, writes Vizenor, "is an active resistance and repudiation of dominance, obtrusive themes of tragedy, ni-
hilism, and victory. The practices of survivance create an active presence, more than the instincts of survival, function, or subsistence."[13]

Introducing his survey text *North American Indian Art*, David W.
Penney foregrounds Vizenor in his discussion of art as a strategy of
Native survival:

> Some Native Americans today criticize museum exhibits,
> popular media, and books like this one, because they often
> situate American Indian culture in a historical past, as if
> there is no Native American culture today. This failure to
> frame the past from the standpoint of the present is par-
> ticularly unfortunate when considering Native American
> arts, since indigenous artists have always been, and are still
> now, among those who most actively reconcile the tradi-
> tions of the past with the circumstances of the present. Art
> is, and has been, one of the principal strategies of Native
> American "survivance," to use Gerald Vizenor's term.[14]

Similar to Berlo and Phillips, Penney attends in his survey text to ways
that Native artists responded to "the historical events of contact, conquest, resistance, and 'survivance.'" In chapters organized by region, or
"culture area," Penney begins with the Ancient Woodlands, where he
emphasizes archeological knowledge, and then opens a new chapter
on the Eastern Woodlands with the first encounters between indigenous peoples and European arrivals. This and subsequent chapters
on the Southwest, the Plains, the West, the Northwest Coast, and the
Arctic—an organization that parallels other survey texts—consider
changes in materials, techniques, and imagery in Native art in response
to contact and colonization; themes of continuity, innovation, adaptation, and resistance; and, countering the presumed anonymity and collective orientation of Native artists, the work of individual artists.

More obviously in their survey, Berlo and Phillips complicate the
narrative of colonial domination, writing, "The many moments of transformation, rupture, and renewal in art contained in this story reveal
the importance of visual arts in maintaining the integrity of spiritual,
social, political, and economic systems."[15] Thus the works by decidedly
contemporary Native artists intervene in the chronological narrative,

asserting continuities of worldviews and cultural traditions. This presence, "against all the historical odds," is a visual manifestation of what Berlo and Phillips term "an emerging post-colonial re-presentation of Aboriginal history and culture."[16] This notion of "post-colonial re-presentation" resides at the core of how we consider the fundamental question of perspective.

It is helpful that Berlo and Phillips call attention to Native art history as a discursive practice throughout their book as they emphasize issues such as the impact of colonialism; the problematic of authenticity; commoditization and patronage; gender; cross-cultural encounters among Native peoples as well as between Native peoples and non-Native newcomers; innovation and tradition; and histories of collecting, ownership, and display of Native American material culture. The authors also address long-standing themes in Native art history: art as an expression of political power, representations of cosmology and spiritual authority, personal adornment, and art as an expression of individual and collective identity.

Utilized in conjunction with survey texts such as Berlo and Phillips's *Native North American Art*, publications such as the National Museum of the American Indian's *All Roads Are Good* are immensely useful in bringing Native voices to the center of our teaching. Published in 1994 in conjunction with the first major exhibit at NMAI's George Gustav Heye Center at the U.S. Custom House in New York City, this compilation of essays by twenty-three indigenous artists, scholars, educators, elders, and community leaders from throughout the Americas offers insight into Native arts in a range of media from a variety of locations. As W. Richard West Jr., citizen of the Cheyenne and Arapaho Tribes of Oklahoma and founding director of the Smithsonian's National Museum of the American Indian, writes in his foreword, "For me, *All Roads Are Good: Native Voices on Life and Culture* represents the important first effort of the National Museum of the American Indian to do precisely what is suggested by the book's title—bring the essential voices of native peoples themselves to the interpretation of our cultures and the things we have made."[17]

The accessible, thoughtful, and engaging essays contained in this volume invite students to consider Native perspectives on questions of intention, aesthetics, materials, function, Native and non-Native encounters, meaning, memory, agency, display, and repatriation—themes that should resonate throughout any class on American Indian art. In the book's preface, the Choctaw and Chippewa historian Clara Sue Kidwell's discussion of jingle dresses begins with her mother's admonition, "You don't mix jingles made from Copenhagen cans with those made from Skoal cans, because the tones of the two don't harmonize." This rule, she says, "underscores the most important dimension of a jingle dress—it is made to be heard as well as seen, and to be heard, it must move."[18] For students accustomed to thinking about Native art as cultural artifacts, Kidwell immediately personalizes the jingle dress and thus foregrounds the question of perspective. Of her great-aunt's jingle dress Kidwell writes, "Even displayed, it would be a static thing, silent and motionless. Chippewa women, viewing this dress as an object on display, can recall the layered meanings attached to this garment as memories of the powwows and of family traditions that determined how dresses were made, by whom, and for what purpose inform their response. The non-Indian, or even non-Chippewa, viewer may see the colorful material, the shiny cones, and the painstaking hand-stitching, but could easily miss the real significance that the dress has."[19]

As they consider past and present forms of artistic expression, the curators and authors of the *All Roads Are Good* exhibition and catalog deter any tendency to romanticize or exoticize Native peoples as "other." Overall, the essays in *All Roads Are Good* comprise contemporary responses to what are, for the most part, ancient and historical objects in the collection of the National Museum of the American Indian. These objects are too often discussed in archeological terms without considering the European-centered paradigms that have shaped this discourse. The examples of art that are discussed in these essays can explicate the material covered in survey texts; in class discussion or written assignments, students can be asked to consider why they think these authors chose particular works of art, how these examples illuminate the points they are making in their essays, and how these readings amplify the students' thinking about issues or themes in Native American art history that are prominent in the survey being used in the course.

As a component of the *All Roads Are Good* exhibition, the Plains Cree artist and curator Gerald McMaster designed a spiral of diverse indigenous cultures' footwear from the NMAI collection that invokes a stately dance. McMaster's essay, "Discovering the Levels of Meaning," focuses on moccasins and other kinds of Native footwear as a metaphor for diversity, movement, ancestral connection, contemporary identity, and survival. "This was a chance to make a hemispheric statement about Native Americans," McMaster writes, "one that suggests the connections between our ancestors and the Native Americans of today."[20] It is important for students to understand that Native cultures—and Native people—are alive and are part of the contemporary world, and that the cultural continuity represented in this exhibit and emphasized in these essays is dynamic, not static, and wonderfully diverse.

NATIVE MODERNISMS

To include Native perspectives in dialogues about Native arts over the past century complicates the question of methodological or theoretical approach, and counters the notion that Native art has served as an influence for European and European American modernism but has not itself engaged and advanced modernist practice. In NMAI's "Native Modernism" symposium, the Tuscarora artist, curator, and writer Jolene Rickard posed provocative and challenging questions about Native artists' relationship to modernism, and, by extension, postmodernism. Rickard asks, "What are the implications of locating Native art within the categorization of modern? If 'modernism' is a theoretical formation of the philosophical West, where does art beyond the 'West' fit? Is Native art beyond the 'West'? As provocative as the rejection of framing Native art as modern can be, is it also strategic to be 'modern'?"[21]

This question of Native artists' strategic engagement with modernism deserves substantial attention in the teaching of Native American art. In their book's final chapter, "The Twentieth Century: Trends in Modern Native Art," Berlo and Phillips address unresolved—and perhaps irresolvable—questions of definition:

> To be judged "modern," must a work be produced in Western media and formats, or should all forms of art made by Native people during the past century be included, whether in "craft" or "fine art" media? If expressed in Western media, must the works deal with "contemporary" issues or should art about traditional heritage and belief be included? Is professional art-school training and familiarity with current idioms of modernism or postmodernism a necessity, or are apprenticeship and the use of historicist styles acceptable? Other unresolved issues also complicate questions of definition. To be judged "Native," must the work be by an artist whose Native status is legally recognized by the U.S. or Canadian government?[22]

While Berlo and Phillips acknowledge the art historical weight of non-Native definitions of modernism, centered on stylistic rejection of illusionism and emphasis on individual self-expression, they focus their consideration of modernism instead on Native artists' "adoption of Western representational styles, genres, and media in order to produce works that function as autonomous entities and that are intended to be experienced independently of community or ceremonial contexts."[23] They emphasize the social and economic circumstances within which Native artists have engaged with non-Native artists and patrons, particularly through consideration of pivotal institutions such as the Santa Fe Indian School's "Studio School," established in 1932, the commoditization of the work of this program's alumni, and the Institute of American Indian Arts, founded thirty years later on the site of the earlier Santa Fe Studio. As well, they examine the various convergences of

Native and non-Native modernisms throughout the twentieth century and the contested meanings of postmodernism for Native artists.

Penney's final chapter in *North American Indian Art*, "Artists of the Modern and Contemporary World," poses the question, "In addition to resistance and adaptation, what of those artists who actively engaged the artistic values of the outsiders in their own terms, appropriating them, challenging them, and, in some cases, transforming them?"[24] He begins this chapter with a consideration of late nineteenth- and early twentieth-century examples of visual auto-ethnography—self-representation by colonized subjects that engages with the colonizer's terms—as a self-conscious strategy of reclamation. As do Berlo and Phillips, Penney also considers ways that twentieth-century artists variously negotiated the expectations of patrons, curators, and educators, as well as their desires for self-expression and communal expectations for the maintenance of cultural traditions. He discusses arts revivals as the impetus for community revitalization, and ways that contemporary Native artists have engaged with representations and misrepresentations of Native Americans, particularly at the time of the Columbus Quincentennial in 1992.

The quincentennial was an occasion for introspection, resistance, subversion, and acts of transformation from observed to participant on the part of Native artists and curators. As the Salish, French-Cree, and Shoshone artist and curator Jaune Quick-to-See Smith wrote in her curator's statement for *The Submoloc Show/Columbus Wohs*, an exhibition organized in response to the celebration of Columbus's arrival in the Caribbean and the destruction and genocide that ensued, "In the midst of struggle for survival, Indian peoples have continued to sustain themselves through the making of art. . . . The hegemony in this celebration has pressured these artists to respond from a gut level to express the anguish they feel. The strength of these Indian voices as this exhibit travels the United States is testimony to the fact that American Indians are alive and well."[25] The fall 1992 issue of *Art Journal*, published by the College Art Association, was devoted to "Recent Native American Art," and the articles in this issue remain relevant to students of contemporary Native art today.[26] An abundance of exhibition catalogs published since 1992 in the United States and Canada similarly document contemporary indigenous art as an ongoing manifestation of cultural vibrancy. Essays by Native American and First Nations artists, curators, and critical theorists contained in these publications, including *Indigena: Contemporary Native Perspectives* (1992), *Watchful Eyes: Native American Women Artists* (1994), and *Reservation X: The Power of Place in Aboriginal Contemporary Art* (1998), are regarded as pivotal in the field.[27] As well, institutions such as the National Museum of the American Indian, the Institute of American Indian Arts, and the Plains Indian Museum at the Buffalo

Bill Historical Center offer comprehensive online resources that foreground Native voices.[28]

Many art historians, anthropologists, curators, critics, and artists writing about recent Native art utilize contemporary theoretical and critical approaches to significant issues in Native art history from the past one hundred years. Essays in the anthology *Native American Art in the Twentieth Century*, edited by W. Jackson Rushing, explore place, community, spirituality, memory, language, indigenous knowledge, sovereignty, and globalization as they problematize fixed notions of identity and authenticity.[29] Since 1999, the Eiteljorg Museum of American Indians and Western Art in Indianapolis has awarded, every two years, five fellowships and one distinguished artist fellowship for lifetime achievement to contemporary Native American and First Nations artists.[30] The First Nations and American Indian writers and artists whose work makes up the catalog *Indigena* variously address what five hundred years of colonization have meant to indigenous people: repatriation as a principle of justice, and self-representation as an assertion of Native presence and agency. As Gerald McMaster and the Mohawk curator and contemporary Native arts scholar Lee-Ann Martin write in their introduction to *Indigena*, "To be an Aboriginal person, to identify with an indigenous heritage in these late colonial times, requires a life of reflection, critique, persistence and struggle."[31]

These and additional examples of recent scholarship and critical texts about twentieth- and twenty-first century Native American art complicate superficial binaries of "traditional" and "modern," and simplistic readings of Native artists' engagement with modernism and postmodernism. In "What More Do They Want?" also published in *Indigena*, the Métis filmmaker and cultural critic Loretta Todd denounces the marginalization of Native voices in the theorizing of modernism and postmodernism. In the absence of indigenous perspectives, she argues, a non-Native worldview is imposed in classifying the work of Native artists as modern or postmodern, and thus misunderstanding of contemporary indigenous art is perpetuated. Todd writes, "What does the use of these terms mean to our cultural production? And what relationships do they have to colonial history, and to our continued struggle with our own territorial and cultural sovereignty?"[32] To counter the detrimental impact of this silencing, Todd asserts the need for recognition of indigenous-based theory: "But what of our own theories of art, our own philosophies of life, our own purposes for representation? By reducing our cultural expression to simply the question of modernism or postmodernism, art or anthropology, or whether we are contemporary or traditional, we are placed on the edges of the dominant culture, while the dominant culture determines whether we are allowed to enter into its realm of art. . . . When we assert our own meanings and philosophies of representation we render the divisions irrelevant, and maintain our Aboriginal right to name ourselves."[33] Claiming this right, Todd calls for dialogue that explores "the to and fro movement" between Native and non-Native cultures, and she emphasizes the critical need for Native voices to be central to a discourse that foregrounds self-naming and indigenous life experiences and knowledge.

Privileging Native voices in teaching and learning about the interactions and various forms of artistic engagement among Native and non-Native artists during the past one hundred years renders inevitable the reconsideration of assumptions—based in colonialist and postcolonial power relations, gender relations, and European-based art historical discourse—that inform canonical narratives of modernism. These include narratives about who is an observer and who is observed, innovation and appropriation, privileged relationships with particular art historical traditions, and the valorization of the individual artist as a technical and stylistic innovator. Scholars such as Todd call these narratives into question and point to potential transformations of the broader meanings of modernism.

NATIVE AMERICAN ART AS WORLD ART

Often, Native American art is one component of courses that focus on the indigenous arts of the "non-West," newly designated as "world art." The idea of "non-Western art history," while intended to broaden the range of art history's historically Eurocentric vision, instead reifies European art as central to art historical discourse and construes the work of non-European artists as "other." Thus it is preferable to designate what a course covers—for example, "Arts of Africa, Oceania, and the Americas"—rather than what it does not. Courses such as these explore various forms of visual expression produced by artists of diverse indigenous cultures. Grounded in art history, world art courses generally incorporate multiple disciplinary perspectives to look at themes in visual expression and cultural production that are relevant across cultures. These include relationships between art, beliefs, cultural values, and social experience; colonial and postcolonial perspectives on representation; aesthetic systems; art and social structure; life passages; and continuity and change. Janet Catherine Berlo and Lee Anne Wilson's *Arts of Africa, Oceania, and the Americas,* a compilation of selected readings in the field, offers just such a thematic approach to the study of art from these areas of the world.[34]

As these courses decenter traditional European American concepts of art and its purposes, they encourage students to reevaluate their own preconceived notions regarding the meanings and functions of art and the relationships between artists and audiences. Often, students enroll in such courses with a desire to understand cultures and creations from outside their own experiences and worldviews. However, deconstructing some of their predetermined concepts can be challenging. Students enter these courses with assumptions regarding quality and value, often believing that European works are the only true "masterpieces" of art. Such suppositions about art have correlations with the ways that students think about people and cultures.

One assumption often made by students is that aesthetics simply concern the artistically "beautiful." In courses on world art, students have opportunities to consider various concepts of beauty that, in contrast to European ideals, often encompass something beyond the final, visually perceived object. As Berlo writes, "For the Navajo artist in the American southwest, aesthetic concepts have far-reaching implications for morality as well as art."[35] Rather than placing full significance on the final artistic product, the process of making art is aesthetically significant to the Navajo/Diné and thus imbues their work with meaning that extends beyond the visual.

For some students, a more difficult topic is the devastation of colonialism in the parts of the world that these courses cover. It is imperative that world art courses address indigenous peoples' shared experiences of colonization, dislocation, assimilation, and genocide. At the same time, these experiences are shaped by the historically specific conditions of each location studied; only within these particular contexts can the visual responses of artists living in these politically charged circumstances be understood. One experience shared by colonized indigenous peoples in various parts of the world is their education in the boarding schools established during the nineteenth century by colonial governments. Fundamental to colonizers' efforts to assimilate indigenous peoples into the dominant culture, boarding schools disrupted families, cultural practices, and individual lives. As Margaret L. Archuleta states in her introduction to the 2000 exhibit catalog *Away from Home: American Indian Boarding School Experiences*, "Indian boarding schools were key components in the process of cultural genocide against Native cultures and were designed to physically, ideologically, and emotionally remove Indian children from their families, homes, and tribal affiliations. From the moment students arrived at school, they could not 'be Indian' in any way—culturally, artistically, spiritually, or linguistically."[36] Particularly important to discussions of historical realities such as boarding schools is consideration of indigenous visual responses, as well as the ways in which images such as photographs of boarding school students were used as propaganda in support of assimilation policies.

While courses in world art can foster multicultural understandings of philosophical ideals from culturally relevant perspectives, their emphasis on cross-cultural confluences and shared experiences can too easily minimize the differences among peoples and arts of various parts of the world. Another conundrum presented by such courses is the idea of "tradition," presumed to be unchanging and created in a timeless past in which no "outside" influences have intruded. A standard—yet now outdated—approach to textbooks formulated for classes such as these presents "traditional" works of art from various locations around the globe that generally predate contact with Europeans. But seldom do they consider changes in visual culture that resulted from subsequent encounters with European arrivals, interactions among dislocated and relocated indigenous peoples, or responses to economic changes and the demands of new markets for indigenous arts. Very rarely are modern and contemporary works given attention in these courses. Reinforcing the idea that "authentic" Native arts are produced only in isolation from outside influences and that colonialism brought about the end of Native American civilizations, world art survey texts often end discussions of Native North American art with the end of the nineteenth century, if not earlier.

However, it is critical that these courses emphasize the agency of indigenous peoples in negotiating cultural change through artistic adaptation and ingenuity, and introduce the idea of "tradition" as dynamic rather than static, encompassing both continuity and change, with attention to shifts in forms, materials, aesthetics, and meanings that result from encounters among Native peoples, and among Native and non-Native peoples. The ongoing realities of intercultural encounter and cultural change that began in ancient times and accelerated with European contact are denied by the prevalent anthropological fantasy of an arbitrary time known as the "ethnographic present" in which "authentic" indigenous arts persist. Independent of Native perspectives, aspects of indigenous art that exemplify continuity from pre-contact times are valorized; Native peoples' negotiations of change, and the manifestations of cultural encounter and contemporary realities in their art, are thus cast outside the discursive boundaries of "non-Western" art because they are perceived as "inauthentic."

Native arts of the Northwest Coast, often presented in world art survey courses, have bridged the gap between the mythic ethnographic present and verifiable contemporary experience. The difference in approach when discussing the art of this area is due in part to the work of Bill Holm, who was the first art historian to articulate in a scholarly way the components of the Northwest Coast formline style and to identify the unique approaches of individual artists to this style.[37] For example, through Holm's essay "Will the Real Charles Edenshaw Please Stand Up?" students learn to recognize both adherence to tradition and stylistic innovation in the works of individual artists.[38] Rather than being seen as frozen in a mythic past, individually named artists are now recognized for their originality and their contributions to the continuity of traditional forms in contemporary Northwest Coast art.

To teach Native American art within courses on North American art demands reconsideration of the canonical discourse of American art history. Along with incorporating Native American material culture into course content, such courses need to interrogate ways that colonialist and postcolonial power relations and ideologies of gender have shaped the trajectories of European and European American art history, and they must expose and problematize the underlying assumptions about artists, artistic innovations, influence, and audience that marginalize the artistic practices of the diverse non-European peoples of this continent. Courses in American art history must take into account works created not only by the European colonizers but also by the indigenous inhabitants of this land, as well as those forcibly brought here. With consideration of the particular historical, political, social, and cultural circumstances in which the art of North America has been produced by diverse peoples, these courses should focus on encounters across cultures, border crossings, and location/dislocation and address questions of ideology, social constructions of gender, race, and class, formulations of "American" identity, and representations of self and "other." Further, these courses must take into account culturally relevant perspectives, including Native perspectives on art produced by Native and non-Native artists.

While most narratives of the history of the art of North America rightly begin with consideration of the ancient art produced by the original inhabitants of this continent, too often Native art is consigned to the margins of these narratives with the arrival of Columbus to the Caribbean. Native peoples, and American Indian art, thus become a prologue to an art history that presumes that the beginning of the true lineage of American art began with the arrival of these Europeans. In addition, the diversity of Native cultures and the range of historical experiences are typically under-scrutinized. The history of art in North America is more correctly a nexus of histories of cross-cultural encounters between diverse peoples. These encounters begin not with the arrival of Europeans but are evident in ancient indigenous arts of the Americas that embody cross-cultural interaction, political and social relations, and artistic influence as well as the effects of displacement and conquest.

With the influx of Europeans, the arts of North America were shaped by interactions among Native Americans and non-Native newcomers, and visual culture played a role in shaping these interactions as well. While many courses on North American art focus on the European and European American artists' visual manifestations of expansion, colonialism, and the establishment of empire, Native visual responses, and Native perspectives on these developments, are too often ignored. Newer survey texts emphasize encounters and interactions between Native and non-Native peoples in North America, and highlight cultural continuities from ancient times to the present. As its title suggests, *American Encounters: Art, History, and Cultural Identity*, coauthored by Angela L. Miller, Janet C. Berlo, Bryan J. Wolf, and Jennifer L. Roberts and published in 2008, looks at multiple forms of encounter—across cultures and among a range of forms of visual and material culture, and explores various constructs of American identity. Throughout this survey text, the authors' emphasis is visual representation of encounters and interactions that shape and are shaped by ideologies of American identity at particular historical moments; their aim is to look anew at how American art history is written. The authors write, "Our theme of encounter not only expands *what* we look at but *how* we look at it."[39] In *Framing America: A Social History of American Art*, Frances K. Pohl draws on the breadth of contemporary scholarship on North American art history, "with an emphasis on developing a critical understanding of how artists, the work they produce, and the critical writings or debates surrounding this work function within specific communities at specific moments in history."[40]

Both of these surveys of the arts of North America position Native American art history as fundamental to their narratives of encounter. And both surveys similarly highlight ways that individual and communal artistic production is embedded in historical circumstances, simultaneously shaped by and helping to shape historically specific social relations and institutional structures. In *American Encounters*, the authors discuss the new images, forms, and materials of Native arts that begin with European contact and highlight the participation of Native peoples of various regions of North America through a global exchange of raw materials and finished goods, concluding with numerous examples of the syncretic forms of expression that resulted. The inclusion of more recent examples of these cultural dynamics, including the work of contemporary mixed-media, performance, and installation artists who have received international notice, calls attention to the historical continuity of Native cultures as well as to the devastation wrought by colonization.

These texts also address the picturing of Native peoples by European artists during the early colonial period, looking at the ways that these images shaped the colonizers' perceptions of the Native peoples they encountered as they moved west. They explore the contested notion of the "frontier"—understood as the edge of the civilized world rather than a border between cultures—the violent encounters that underlay the "nation building" of the eighteenth and nineteenth centuries, the development of a European American visual iconography of nationhood, and the role of images of Native Americans as integral to this visual articulation of "American" identity. Both texts devote considerable attention to nineteenth-century images of landscape and the depiction of Native Americans in nature and *as* nature, signifying both place and, in visual narratives of Manifest Destiny, displacement.

But what of Native artists' engagement with themes of place and displacement? To facilitate students' understanding of the complex historical and psychic underpinnings of the representations of land and home place that are central to Native visual expression, the military confrontations, forced removals, U.S. government assimilationist policies, and prevailing ideologies of the "noble savage" and the "vanishing Indian" must be addressed in teaching Native arts of the nineteenth century. The deliberate confluence of these devastating strategies of conquest is the context in which Native peoples struggled for cultural self-preservation and resisted annihilation. As the authors write in *American Encounters*, "Native artistic traditions throughout these decades paradoxically flourished, showing a technical and artistic inventiveness born of new threats to their cultural identity."[41] The American art survey texts *Framing America* and *American Encounters* give attention to Native representations of the disastrous consequences of U.S. expansion in ledger drawings from the Plains, particularly drawings made by Native men incarcerated at Fort Marion from 1875 to 1878. Drawing attention to the power of visual representation, pivotal images from this period invariably provoke discussion of Native peoples' experiences of displacement and cultural genocide and their negotiation of this historical moment as a practice of resistance and survival.[42]

Twentieth-century American art history often construes Native American art merely as a source for European American experiments in modernist abstraction, and as a signifier of Americanness rooted in the fantasy of indigenous people's harmonious preindustrial coexistence of with the American landscape. But Native American art also plays a key role in these moments in American art history. In "America's Pueblo Artists: Encounters on the Borderlands," David W. Penney and Lisa A. Roberts more fully explicate early twentieth-century encounters among Native American painters from the American Southwest with non-Native patrons. Penney and Roberts explore how Native artists engaged the mainstream art world of early U.S. modernism, arguing that limited understandings of Native paintings—for example, as representations of either "authentic" indigenous identity or assimilated and inauthentic identity—make it difficult to comprehend these works as the product of "dialogic relationships" among these artists and the promoters and consumers of their art.[43] In *Native Moderns: American Indian Painting, 1940–1960*, Bill Anthes looks at the work of the next generation of Native American artists that was both stylistically related to European American modernism and expressive of contemporary Native experiences, but which was perceived at the time as neither sufficiently modern nor authentically "Indian." "The crossing over and

self-fashioning of twentieth-century Native American artists suggests
a larger story of American modernism than is usually recounted in
academic art history," writes Anthes, as he asserts the integral place of
these artists in narratives of American modernism.[44]

Despite the outwardly modernist experimentation of mid-century
Native painters, these artists are often left out of histories of American
abstraction, in which Native art figures only as inspiration for European
American painters. In addressing how European American artists both
gained artistic insight from Native painters and also overtly appropriated imagery from Native arts, courses in North American art should
also address the participation of Native artists in movements such as abstract expressionism, pop art, minimalism, and conceptual art, in order
to understand Native work contextually, and as simultaneously Native
and modern.

Even in recent North American art survey texts, Native art of the
latter part of the twentieth century is represented only in the context
of multicultural expressions of identity. The only mention of a Native
artist in *American Encounters* in the section on art from 1960 to 1980 is a
discussion of the Kiowa painter T. C. Cannon's *Osage with Van Gogh* or
Collector #5 (1975) as an example of an artist dismantling stereotypes.
As the lone example of the Native artist achieving "rapprochement
between two worlds" and "inverting the expected ethnicities of collector and collected,"[45] by virtue of its singular placement, this now-
iconic image ironically reinforces the essentializing assumptions that
Cannon intended to critique. In the section of *Framing America* titled
"Art and the Politics of Identity," Pohl also discusses art by people of
color in the United States who have been systematically excluded from
mainstream arts institutions and from the discourse of American art
history, emphasizing these artists' "redefinition of the term 'American'
and investigations into the multiple identities within which they lived
and worked."[46] The sole work of art by a Native artist from the second
half of the twentieth century included in this book, Jaune Quick-to-See
Smith's *Trade (Gifts for Trading Land with White People)* of 1992 represents,
in Pohl's words, "visual testimony to the long history of misrepresentations of Native Americans in American culture and their attempts to
counter such misrepresentations."[47]

However, the complexities of twentieth-century Native artists'
engagement with modernism and postmodernism, and with questions
of subjectivity, representations of place, and the construction and negotiation of "American" identity that are at play throughout these most
recent surveys, are virtually absent in these texts' considerations of
contemporary art. In their concluding chapter, "American Art in Flux:
1980–Present," the *American Encounters* authors discuss globalization
and international connections among artists, including postmodernist
strategies such as pastiche and appropriation and the use of text and

language to interrogate practices of communication. The final image in *American Encounters* is from the Tuscarora artist, writer, and curator Jolene Rickard's mixed-media installation *Corn Blue Room* (1998–99), an image that addresses issues of Native sovereignty, indigenous knowledge, cultural and industrial power, genetic engineering, and the ongoing challenges of intercultural encounter. In their conclusion, the authors recall their introduction to the initial encounters between European and Native American cultures, writing, "Rickard's work attests to the fact that this early encounter was not to be a single, isolated event, but rather the inauguration of an ongoing series of complex cultural negotiations."[48] This closing placement of Rickard's work illuminates the continuity of Native responses to cultural encounters and highlights the ways that Native artists continue to negotiate Native identity utilizing indigenous theoretical constructs and contemporary visual language.

**NATIVE ART AS
CONTEMPORARY ART**

Native art belongs in courses on contemporary art. Often organized thematically, these courses generally encompass the study of some combination of new media, subjectivity, appropriation, text and language, representations of the body, artists' relationships to various art historical traditions, and cross-cultural encounters. But, as do surveys of North American art, too many contemporary art courses continue to marginalize or only provisionally include Native artists in their curriculum. These courses should be looking at how Native artists engage contemporary themes and practices, and the role of Native art historical scholarship in the field of contemporary art studies. It is imperative that any course in contemporary art taught in the twenty-first century facilitate students' exploration of art by artists of various ethnicities, approached from culturally relevant perspectives.

The exhibition catalogs, online resources, and "contemporary" sections of survey texts on Native American art discussed above are useful sources for teaching and for student research on contemporary Native art practice, as these provide both images and information about artists. They also offer Native perspectives and theoretical approaches to contemporary issues that emerge from Native worldviews.

**INCORPORATING
INDIGENOUS-BASED THEORIES:
LAND AND HOME PLACE**

Native perspectives on land, and the relationships of indigenous peoples to home places, are crucial to understanding the weight of displacement caused by colonialism and the importance of home place as central to indigenous identity and survival. Recent exhibition catalogs are excellent resources for students' investigation of these perspectives and theoretical constructs. In the exhibition catalog *Reservation X* (1998), seven artists and four writers explore meanings of place, community, and identity for contemporary indigenous peoples. *Who Stole the Tee Pee?* an exhibition at the NMAI (2000), looks at visual representations of indigenous subjectivity, education, commoditization of Native culture, and humor and irony in Native art as they circulate around the theme of home place.[49] *Lifeworlds—Artscapes: Contemporary Iroquois Art* (2003) foregrounds land and home, and examines the ways that contemporary Iroquois artists visually articulate a sense of place and what it means to be Iroquois in the contemporary world.[50] *Off the Map: Landscape in the Native Imagination* (2007) is an exploration of Native relationships to physical, psychic, metaphorical, and imaginary landscapes. In this catalog, the Navajo curator Kathleen Ash-Milby writes about contemporary Native people's relationships to the land and to historical representations of landscape, as well as ways that contemporary Native artists have articulated these relationships. Recognizing that landscape is "a genre of painting dominated by European conventions," she argues that Native images of geographic and metaphorical landscapes are "inherently indigenous":

> Geography has shaped and defined our cultures, literally
> and conceptually, over countless generations. Our origin
> stories and understanding of the universe often relate
> to features of the landscape. . . . The material culture of
> our communities is based on the natural resources of our
> homelands. . . . For more than 500 years, land has also
> been a site and source of conflict and struggle with out-
> siders, be they non-Indian settlers seeking farmland or
> commercial enterprises eager to exploit natural resources.
> As a subject for Native artists, the land/landscape is laden
> with history and expectation. Land is home, culture, and
> identity, but it also represents violence, isolation, and loss.[51]

Ash-Milby's essay is particularly useful for teaching the meanings of landscape across cultures in the visual iconography of the United States. She discusses ways that iconic depictions of landscape by non-Native artists discussed in North American art survey texts, such as Albert Bierstadt's *The Rocky Mountains, Lander's Peak* (1863), served ideological and political purposes, encouraging immigration and justifying colonialist expansion and exploitation of the land. Of the landscape painters of the American West who worked in the manner of the Hudson River School, Ash-Milby writes, "Their breathtaking vistas reinforced the myth of the empty frontier, bestowed upon Euro-American settlers and entrepreneurs for exploitation through Manifest Destiny. . . . The Native presence in the art of this era is most notable for its absence."[52] But Ash-Milby also considers the ways that Native artists have subverted this paradigm, how they have inverted colonialist power relations, and ultimately how these artists have created potent counter-narratives of North American history. She concludes her essay with the following observation:

> If it is possible to slip a definition around the idea of Native landscape, it may be with the words "multiplicity" and "ambiguity." These words encompass the complexity of contemporary indigenous experience with land and the idea of landscape, as well as the futility of attempting to delineate its borders. The traditional understanding of the land is far more nuanced and multidimensional than can be expressed through simple representation. . . .
>
> To fully appreciate what these artists do, we must re-examine our biases and assumptions and recognize that the diasporic and culturally syncretic sensibilities expressed here represent a very real contemporary Native experience. For Native people the relationship between the self and the land/the artist and the landscape will always be fraught with emotion and the weight of history and belief.[53]

Essays such as this are valuable for students of Native American art because they emphasize indigenous perspectives on land and ways that these perspectives infuse contemporary Native artists' engagement with landscape—a prevalent theme in art practice and scholarship.

CONCLUSION: TEACHING AND LEARNING

In teaching Native American art, class discussions, written assignments, and group projects can be designed to hone students' ability to analyze source material in terms of scholarly validity, perspective, and voice, and to facilitate students' formulation of and engagement with increasingly complex questions. These activities can also encourage students to reflect deeply on the meanings of specific works of art for their makers, for their cultures of origins, for subsequent viewers—and for the students themselves.

But many non-Native students inevitably come to these courses because they are attracted to romanticized images of Native Americans and their art. It is troublesome when non-Native students attempt to express in visual form their affinity for Native art through "Indian" materials, imagery, and styles. One way to address such inappropriate appropriation is to discuss intention and artistic influence in the context of previous class discussions of power, representation, and voice, and then to ask students to produce visual responses to what they have learned during the course. In our teaching, we have assigned final projects in which students are required to engage self-reflectively with questions they found particularly meaningful, to make a work of art in response to these questions, and to write a short essay about how the art they produced related to their learning and, finally, how they thought about the question of appropriation as they created this work of art.

In teaching Native American art in any art history courses, it is crucial to listen to the voices of Native artists and scholars and to privilege these voices as fundamental to our teaching and our students' learning. Attending to Native perspectives can help to elucidate layers of meaning in ways that can complement, complicate, challenge, or contradict students' previous assumptions about American Indian art and art history. This is an issue particularly for non-Native scholars and educators. Colonization denies history, identity, and voice. It demands that those who are its target speak the language of the dominant culture, in ways that are acceptable to this culture. Colonized peoples who are forced to assimilate not only have to grapple with new ways of learning languages, but, more insidiously, new ways of thinking through this new language. It is imperative that non-Native educators teaching about Native art do not *speak for* the artists whose work we represent in our classrooms, but instead facilitate students' access to Native perspectives on this art. All students in these courses need to understand why it is important to learn about Native arts through the perspectives of Native scholars and artists who are authorities on this art and the history and experiences that inform it. To cede authoritative primacy to Native voices in teaching and learning Native American art history and to structure our courses in alignment with Native worldviews must be an intentional intellectual praxis.

Melanie Anne Herzog is professor of art history at Edgewood College in Madison, Wisconsin. She is the author of *Elizabeth Catlett: An American Artist in Mexico* (2000) and *Milton Rogovin: The Making of a Social Documentary Photographer* (2006). Additional publications include "Women of Metal: Innovation, Connection, and Education" in *Women of Metal* (2008); "Telling Untold Stories," in *Flo Oy Wong: Whispers of the Past*, an exhibition catalog published by the 40 Acres Gallery in Sacramento, California, in 2007; and "Dancing in Two Worlds: The Portraits of Tom Jones," in *Wisconsin People and Ideas* (2006).

Sarah Anne Stolte is a PhD candidate at the University of Wisconsin–Madison. She assisted with the exhibition and symposium *Epicentro: Retracing the Plains*, presented during the vernissage of the Venice Biennale, June 1–4, 2011, and was the Paul Dyck Plains Indian Museum Collections intern at the Buffalo Bill Historical Center in Cody, Wyoming, during the summer of 2011.

NOTES

1 On the formative years of the field of Native American art history, see Janet Catherine Berlo, ed., *The Early Years of Native American Art History: The Politics of Scholarship and Collecting* (Seattle: University of Washington Press, 1992). For a thoughtful discussion of the location of Native American art history within the academy, see Joyce M. Szabo, "Native American Art History: Questions of the Canon," in *Essays on Native Modernism: Complexity and Contradiction in American Indian Art* (Washington: National Museum of the American Indian, Smithsonian Institution, 2006), 69–87. This volume was published following a symposium on the subject of Native modernism held at NMAI in Washington in spring of 2005, which was offered in conjunction with this institution's inaugural exhibition of work by George Morrison and Allan Houser; see Truman T. Lowe, ed., *Native Modernism: The Art of George Morrison and Allan Houser* (Washington: National Museum of the American Indian, Smithsonian Institution, 2004).

2 W. Jackson Rushing, "Critical Issues in Recent Native American Art," *Art Journal* 51, no. 3 (1992): 13.

3 For a more thorough consideration of this history, see Berlo, *Early Years of Native American Art History.*

4 On the marketing of Native art at the turn of the twentieth century, see various essays in Berlo, *Early Years of Native American Art History.*

5 See Melanie Herzog, "Aesthetics and Meanings: The Arts and Crafts Movement and the Revival of American Indian Basketry," in *The Substance of Style: Perspectives on the American Arts and Crafts Movement*, ed. Bert Denker (Winterthur, Del.: Henry Francis du Pont Winterthur Museum, 1996), 69–91.

6 See Marvin Cohodas, "Louisa Keyser and the Cohns: Mythmaking and Basket Making in the American West," in Berlo, *Early Years of Native American Art History*, 88–133; and Marvin Cohodas, "Washoe Innovators and Their Patrons," in *The Arts of the North American Indian: Native Traditions in Evolution*, ed. Edwin L. Wade (New York: Hudson Hills Press, 1986), 203–20.

7 *The Language of Native American Baskets*, National Museum of the American Indian, Smithsonian Institution, http://nmai.si.edu/exhibitions/baskets/.

8 John Haworth, "On the Map," in *Off the Map: Landscape in the Native Imagination* (Washington: National Museum of the American Indian, Smithsonian Institution, 2007), 12.

9 Kay WalkingStick, "Native American Art in the Postmodern Era," *Art Journal* 51, no. 3 (1992): 16.

10 Janet Catherine Berlo and Ruth B. Phillips, *Native North American Art* (Oxford: Oxford University Press, 1998), 3.

11 Ibid.

12 Ibid.

13 Gerald Vizenor, "Aesthetics of Survivance: Literary Theory and Practice," in *Survivance: Narratives of Native Presence*, ed. Gerald Vizenor (Omaha: University of Nebraska Press, 2008), 11.

14 David W. Penney, *North American Indian Art* (London: Thames and Hudson, 2004), 10.

15 Berlo and Phillips, *Native North American Art*, 4.

16 Ibid.

17 W. Richard West, Jr., "Foreword," in *All Roads Are Good: Native Voices on Life and Culture* (Washington: National Museum of the American Indian, Smithsonian Institution, 1994), 9.

18 Clara Sue Kidwell, "Preface," in *All Roads Are Good*, 14.

19 Ibid.

20 Gerald McMaster, "Discovering the Levels of Meaning," in *All Roads Are Good*, 116.

21 Jolene Rickard is quoted in Bruce Bernstein and Truman T. Lowe, "New Horizons," in *Essays on Native Modernism*, 24.

22 Berlo and Phillips, *Native North American Art*, 209.

23 Ibid., 210.

24 Penney, *North American Indian Art*, 189.

25 Jaune Quick-to-See Smith, "Curator's Statement," in *The Submoloc Show/Columbus Wohs: A Visual Commentary on the Columbus Quincentennial from the Perspective of America's First People* (Phoenix: Atlatl, 1992), iii.

26 *Art Journal* 51, no. 3 (1992), guest editors W. Jackson Rushing and Kay WalkingStick.

27 See Gerald McMaster and Lee-Ann Martin, eds., *Indigena: Contemporary Native Perspectives* (Hull, Quebec: Canadian Museum of Civilization, 1992); Theresa Harlan and Jolene Rickard, eds., *Watchful Eyes: Native American Women Artists* (Phoenix: Heard Museum, 1994); and Gerald McMaster, ed., *Reservation X: The Power of Place in Aboriginal Contemporary Art* (Hull, Quebec: Canadian Museum of Civilization, 1998).

28 See National Museum of the American Indian, Smithsonian Institute, http://www.nmai.si.edu/; Plains Indian Museum, Buffalo Bill Historical Center, http://www.bbhc.org/explore/plains-indians/; and Institute of American Indian Arts, http://www.iaia.org/.

29 W. Jackson Rushing, ed., *Native American Art in the Twentieth Century: Makers, Meanings, Histories* (London: Routledge, 1999). On mid-twentieth century Native American art, see also Bill Anthes, *Native Moderns: American Indian Painting, 1940–1960* (Durham: Duke University Press, 2006).

30 To date, seven catalogs of work by recipients of the Eiteljorg Fellowship for Native American Fine Art have been published by the Eiteljorg Museum of American Indians and Western Art (after the first volume, these have been published in association with University of Washington Press): *Contemporary Masters* (1999), *After the Storm* (2001), *Path Breakers* (2003), *Into the Fray* (2005), *Diversity and Dialogue* (2007), *Art Quantum* (2009), and *We Are Here* (2011). Also see the Eiteljorg Fellowship Web site, http://www.fellowship.eiteljorg.org/.

31 Gerald McMaster and Lee-Ann Martin, "Introduction," in McMaster and Martin, *Indigena,* 11. Also in this volume, on the critical importance of repatriation, see Gloria Cranmer Webster, "From Colonization to Repatriation," 25–37.

32 Loretta Todd, "What More Do They Want?" in McMaster and Martin, *Indigena,* 73.

33 Ibid., 75.

34 See Janet Catherine Berlo and Lee Anne Wilson, eds., *Arts of Africa, Oceania, and the America: Selected Readings* (Englewood Cliffs, N.J.: Prentice Hall, 1993).

35 Janet Catherine Berlo, "Aesthetic Systems: Knowledge, Beauty, and Power," in Berlo and Wilson, *Arts of Africa, Oceania, and the America,* 2.

36 Margaret Archuleta, "Introduction," in *Away from Home: American Indian Boarding School Experiences,* ed. Margaret Archuleta, Brenda J. Child, and K. Tsianina Lomawaima (Phoenix: Heard Museum, 2000), 19.

37 The first of Holm's numerous publications on Northwest Coast art that transformed the field is *Northwest Coast Indian Art: An Analysis of Form* (Seattle: University of Washington Press, 1965).

38 Bill Holm, "Will the Real Charles Edenshaw Please Stand Up? The Problem of Attribution in Northwest Coast Indian Art," in Berlo and Wilson, *Arts of Africa, Oceania, and the Americas,* 86–110.

39 Angela L. Miller, Janet C. Berlo, Bryan J. Wolf, and Jennifer L. Roberts, *American Encounters: Art, History, and Cultural Identity* (Upper Saddle River, N.J.: Pearson, 2008), xii.

40 Frances K. Pohl, *Framing America: A Social History of American Art,* 2nd ed. (New York: Thames and Hudson, 2008), 11.

41 Miller et al., *American Encounters,* 222.

42 In *Wohaw Between Two Worlds,* illustrated in *American Encounters,* the Kiowa artist Wohaw shows himself literally and metaphorically with a foot in both worlds, extending peace pipes to a wild buffalo on one side of the drawing and a domesticated steer on the other. The internal and cultural conflict he feels is clear; while he faces the non-Native settlers' wooden frame house and farm field, the sun, crescent moon, and falling star locate the Kiowa realm in relation to larger cosmological forces. The image with which Pohl concludes her discussion of this clash of Native and non-Native worlds as a critical aspect of nineteenth century American national identity is Frances Benjamin Johnston's photograph "Class in American History," circa 1900, in which a young man in Plains regalia is on display for the African American and Native American students who were brought to Hampton Institute (now Hampton University) for an education designed to assimilate them into the social and vocational norms and practices of the dominant culture, the success of which is represented by their dress and demeanor. See Miller et al., *American Encounters,* 313; and Pohl, *Framing America,* 248–50.

43 See David W. Penney and Lisa A. Roberts, "America's Pueblo Artists: Encounters on the Borderlands," in Rushing, *Native American Art in the Twentieth Century,* 21–38. Their work complicates earlier scholarship in this area; see J.J. Brody, *Indian Painters and White Patrons* (Albuquerque: University of New Mexico Press, 1971); and Brody's subsequent *Pueblo Indian Painting: Tradition and Modernism in*

New Mexico, 1900–1930 (Santa Fe: School for Advanced Research Press, 1997).

44 Anthes, *Native Moderns*, xii.

45 Miller et al., *American Encounters*, 611.

46 Pohl, *Framing America*, 551.

47 Ibid.

48 Miller et al., *American Encounters*, 655.

49 Fred Nahwooksy and Richard Hill Sr., *Who Stole the Tee Pee?* (Phoenix: Atlatl, 2000). This exhibition was organized by Atlatl, Inc. and hosted by the National Museum of the American Indian.

50 Sylvia S. Kasprycki and Doris I. Stambrau, eds., *Lifeworlds— Artscapes: Contemporary Iroquois Art* (Frankfurt, Germany: Museum der Weltkulturen, 2003).

51 Kathleen Ash-Milby, "The Imaginary Landscape," in *Off the Map*, 17. See also *Our Land/Ourselves: American Indian Contemporary Artists*, guest curator Jaune Quick-to-See Smith, essays by Paul Brach, Richard W. Hill, Sr., and Lucy R. Lippard (Albany: University Art Gallery, State University of New York, Albany, 1991).

52 Kathleen Ash-Milby, "Imaginary Landscape," 21.

53 Ibid., 45.

No Word for Art in Our Language?
Old Questions, New Paradigms

Nancy Marie Mitblo

Contemporary American Indian art, like other American Indian disciplinary fields, such as American Indian literature, law, or politics, has a unique historical trajectory. Yet unlike these more established scholarly subfields, American Indian art lacks a discernable infrastructure, a theoretical basis, or a comprehensive history.[1] Why is this so, when the arts occupy such an integral space in imagining American Indian identities—past and future? Curator Margaret Archuleta and law scholar Rennard Strickland attribute the failed policies of cultural genocide in America to the power of Native art, concluding that "the determined effort to destroy Indian culture and break Indian pride" failed due to the great legacies of Native American artists who enabled an understanding and preservation of unique cultural traditions.[2] Given the absolute saturation of images and icons surrounding American Indian life and the very real impact of the arts for Native survival, an accounting for the marginalization of Native arts is essential. The underdevelopment of a theoretical basis for American Indian arts both in the realm of public culture (museums and galleries) as well as in established scholarly institutions (universities, publishing industries, and granting institutions) needs to be addressed.[3] Concurrent with this project of unearthing the nominal presence and overwhelming absences of American Indian arts scholarship, attention should be paid to the flux and variations of Native arts reception over time.

My essay examines what I consider three key strategies employed in articulating the place of Indian arts in the broad theoretical land-scape of Indigenous studies internationally: (1) the rejection of standard fine arts categories of reception ("No word for art in my language"); (2) the assimilation of these same fine arts categories ("I'm an artist first and an Indian second," now expressed as a "post-Indian" sensibility); and (3) the creation of new categories that reflect Indigenous values of cultural reclamation, sovereignty, and land-based philosophies (what I term "American Indian Curatorial Practice"). These strategies may in-dependently occur in space (tribal land bases, urban regions) and time (across generations of practitioners). The rejection, incorporation, and creation of the platforms outlined above may be clearly defined by dis-cussion of specific cultural events and places. While I will endeavor to illustrate each of these strategies with an exemplary case study, this nar-rative can only suggest the outlines of the applied and academic work that will hopefully take shape in the careers of our emerging curators and scholars. Only one theorist or school of thought cannot accomplish the crafting of a field of study. This is work that will take generations of events, contemplation, and establishment of patterning to discern.

My analytical approach to the development of contemporary Native arts from the 1960s onward is an effort to amend problematic theories while identifying new applications.[4] Theories, like objects, are flexible, and can be mobilized to speak at will to the concerns of the maker (the artist), the viewer (the audience), or the subject (the indi-vidual or community represented within the artwork). This essay will first examine the orientation of producing artists and then will apply various art projects as evidence of theory.

NO WORD

The Indigenous rejection of fine arts as a descriptor for contemporary American Indian arts is best illustrated by the common refrain "There is no word for art in my language." Native artists and curators expressed this perspective most commonly in the multicultural era of the "new museology," dating roughly from the late 1970s to the early 1990s. The arts commentator and writer Jamake Highwater expressed the "no word" sentiment in his book *The Primal Mind*, in which he observes, "For primal peoples . . . the relationship between experience and expres-sion has remained so direct and spontaneous that they usually do not possess a word for art." Highwater adds, "We cannot readily translate Indian iconography and visions into terms that make realistic sense to the Western mind."[5] Highwater was later exposed as an alleged ethnic fraud for posing as an American Indian when his heritage is reported to have been Italian. Nonetheless, Highwater's manifesto gained credence over time.[6] Throughout the 1980s and into the quincentennial era, the catchphrase was used to express the alienation Native artists experienced in fine arts contexts. In his article "No Word for Art in Tewa Language—Only Meaning," the San Ildefonso ceramicist Lorenzo Gonzales stated, "In non-Indian terms, I'm an artist. In the Tewa world, they say of me, 'He's a very skilled person. He knows many things.'"[7] Likewise, the Navajo artist Leatrice Mikkelsen commented in 1992, "In the language of the Dineh, there is no word for art. When I learned this, I laughed. I was so relieved. This word, and all that it drags with it, was not necessary."[8] The "no word" orientation was reified in the Oxford History of Art series, in which Janet Catherine Berlo and Ruth B. Phillips observe, "When speaking of historical Native objects, the statement is often made that Native languages have no exact equivalent for the post-Renaissance Western term 'art,'" noting that "in Native traditions the purely material and visual features of an object are not necessarily the most important in establishing its relative value, as they have come to be in the West."[9] Thus art historians and Native artists appear to agree that "no word for art in my language" is both accurate and significant. Yet is it possible for both groups to subscribe to this same philosophical standpoint but express differing interpretations of its meaning?

From one perspective, the "no word for art" descriptor indicates an Indigenous rejection of how Native arts are perceived in non-Native contexts such as museums, cultural centers, galleries, and scholarly texts—contexts that imbue fine arts with the Western values of individualism, commercialism, objectivism, and competition, as framed by an elitist point of reference. A rejection of the term "art" is then a rejection of Western culture as capitalist, patriarchal, and, ultimately, shallow, one that does not value the central principles of Indigenous identity, such as land, language, family, and spirituality. A refusal to be co-opted into a more narrow definition of what is an intrinsically more holistic enterprise is also a refusal to be named. It is an effort toward self-determination. This is certainly the orientation of the two Native artists quoted above, Mikkelsen and Gonzales.

This distinction between the naming and the named is of course a distinction of power—who controls the avenues of expression and communication. In the context of the arts industry, museums and galleries are essential components of nationalistic and colonial projects that define and disseminate subjective versions of history and reality. The very real legacy of viewing Indigenous peoples as property, whose bodies and ceremonial items could be collected and curated as archaeological resources, defines this power dynamic. Legislation protecting American Indian bodies and resources was enacted in 1978 with the American Indian Religious Freedom Act, as well as the Archaeological Resources Protection Act of 1979, but it was not until the Native American Graves Protection and Repatriation Act of 1990 (NAGPRA) that a more humanistic approach to the museum enterprise was fully in place. NAGPRA provided a means for Native peoples to dispute the ownership of human remains, sacred objects, and objects of cultural patrimony. American Indians became central players in the massive shift from older museum models of exclusion to the "new museology," where subject voices—those known collectively as cultural others—were the central agents of change, including feminists, and ethnic, religious, racial, and other minority groups.[10] Scholar Julia Harrison argues that the new museum was "driven by the local community: social subjects and concerns replaced objects as its focus."[11]

For politicians like Senator Daniel Inouye, who introduced NAGPRA to Congress, it was not a matter of access or power that was at stake in the new museology, but rather "a basic issue of human rights." Inouye, cochairman of the Senate Select Committee on Indian Affairs, observed, "When human remains are displayed in museums or historical societies, it is never the bones of white soldiers or the first European settlers that came to this continent that are lying in glass cases. It is Indian remains. The message that this sends to the rest of the world is that Indians are culturally and physically different from and inferior to non-Indians. This is racism. . . . The bill [NAGPRA] is not about the validity of museums or the value of scientific inquiry. Rather, it is about human rights."[12]

The movement toward inclusion in museums nationally and globally found a particular resonance in debates concerning American Indian arts. Native arts could no longer be considered purely for their formal or decorative attributes, but rather served more accurately as expressions of cultural patrimony. The ownership of American Indian material culture shifted from the connoisseurship model to a more dynamic, present, and immediate matter of cultural survival, dignity, and sovereignty. In these scenarios, "no word for art in my language" is a political call to action, or as some might claim, a separatist agenda in which the primary frame of reference is not a Western concept but one that originates from an Indigenous cosmology and worldview.

The "no word" rejection can also be interpreted as a hesitation for Indian artists and their supporters to expose their participation in Western art institutions. In the market-saturated era of the 1980s, some Native artists were quick to distance themselves from the Western attributes of upper-class consumption. Crass commercialism signaled an inauthenticity that could actually negate sales by threatening to invalidate the presentation of Native art as spiritually oriented and free of Western influences.[13] The mixed-heritage Inupiak artist Erica Lord defines this type of cultural reappropriation as an orientalizing discourse: "Reappropriation of the culture—You do see that so much in Native art where Indians seem to orientalize their own culture and make it exotic themselves. And you see it all over the place. You see it in Santa Fe *definitely* because that's what sells. And I think there needs to be a competent questioning of who and why and your intent of using these images or these parts of your culture and what you are doing with them."[14]

An artist's denial of economic motivation in Native fine arts settings in an effort to conform to audience expectations becomes another form of playing Indian. While appearing to be politically progressive on the surface, this stance is actually deeply conformist. Rather than conveying the complexities of contemporary Native life, in which sacred and secular interests actively push against each other, this masking of economic complicity maintains a status quo idealization of Indianness at odds with a globalized, mechanized economy.

An opportunistic version of the "no word for art in my language" orientation is decidedly not politically progressive in that it embraces false notions of American Indians as "pure product"—unchanging and dissociated from mainstream realities, such as technology or popular culture.[15] A sense of fragility is suggested in the idea that associations with outside norms can cause traditional values to disintegrate. The Seneca curator Tom Hill states, "We native peoples have idealized ourselves. We tend to think that our worldview is pristine, untouched, uninfluenced by European culture. And that's not true. In any kind of living culture, that culture is constantly changing and evolving."[16]

Another construct is provided by Sally Price, who observes that the category "art" is a convenient and exclusively Western construct, for it gives westerners complete control over the aesthetic judgment of the world's art. Westerners are then freed from the "laborious task" of determining and acknowledging individual ownership or the need to take Native aesthetic frameworks seriously.[17] The liberty westerners take in speaking for Native artists, justified in the belief that Native languages do not have a word for art, is exemplified even in sympathetic appraisals of Native arts, such as Christian Feest's *Native Arts of North America*: "None of the native languages of North America seem to contain a word that can be regarded as synonymous with the Western concept of art, which is usually seen as something separable from the rest of daily life." Feest outlines four kinds of Native art: tribal, ethnic, pan-Indian, and Indian mainstream.[18]

This dispensing with Indigenous categories of reception goes both ways, however, especially when Native artists not only reject Western categories, but also fail to provide alternative references or ideological frameworks. A reluctance to articulate an alternative arts theory in the English language (as Highwater claims above, "We cannot readily translate Indian iconography and visions into terms that make realistic sense to the Western mind") ultimately leads to confusion. It also fosters a dangerous and inaccurate belief that Native artists are unreflective about their own art production or that they lack clear aesthetic criteria.[19] This anti-intellectual agenda imposed on Native arts is a pervasive and as yet undocumented occurrence in Indigenous contexts. As a student and later a faculty member at the Institute of American Indian Arts tribal college, I met students who claimed that arts instruction was unnecessary, that all they really needed were the tools to make art. This "Indians are naturally good artists" stance smacks of internalized racism, similar to the belief that African Americans naturally dance well or that Asians are naturally good at math.

A rejection of art as an established category found favor in the 1980s, but for very different reasons. First, as a separatist claim to Indigeneity, the politically charged era of Indian rights legislation supported "no word for art" perspectives. Second, in the gluttonous decorative Indian arts market in regional settings such as Santa Fe, "no word for art" enabled the crafting of a sellable authentic Indian artist and artwork, untainted by modernist desires. Third, in the "new museology" era of cultural institutions serving unique constituents, "no word for art" signaled an embrace of multiculturalism and difference. And fourth, according to Price, "no word for art" released scholars from the obligation to take Native knowledge systems into consideration, an assumption that even Native scholars and artists adopted. Ward Churchill, another alleged ethnic Indian fraud writer, has claimed, "'Art,' like 'philosophy' and 'religion,' is not an American Indian concept. It is a notion and a category of activity imported from Europe right along with the horse, firearms, trade beads and smallpox. In this sense, contemporary efforts to define what is traditional American Indian art and who are legitimate Americans are more than passingly absurd."[20] While each of these manifestations of the "no word" phenomenon proved remarkably flexible in meeting varying constituents' needs, none propelled the development of scholarship, offering as they did confusing and conflicted meanings for both the buying public and the academic community.

ARTIST FIRST

Incorporation of fine arts signifiers ("I'm an artist first and an Indian second") similarly serves varying needs and communities. This Native arts slogan gained currency in the same 1980s era as "no word for art," yet its life span was extended by postmodern sensibilities that rejected rigid identity concepts as oppressive. The idea of hybridity—a happy melding of cultures or even a transcendence of culture—is currently reflected in the associated term "post-Indian."[21]

The examples I have selected to illustrate the "artist first" ideology are the 2008 exhibitions featuring the work of the late Luiseno painter Fritz Scholder, held concurrently at the Smithsonian National Museum of the American Indian in Washington, D.C., and New York (curated by Truman Lowe and Paul Chaat Smith), and a parallel exhibition at the Institute of American Indian Arts Museum (*Fritz Scholder: An Intimate Look*, curated by Joseph Sanchez). An abstract expressionist painter, Scholder is famous for simultaneously embracing and rejecting his Native identity, stating, "I'm very proud of being a quarter Luiseño, but you can't be anything if you are a quarter."[22] Government-enacted blood quantum policies are mocked in his denial of Native influence altogether. In essence, Scholder actively justifies government recognition of Native populations by collapsing his artistic cultural influences and interests with state policies that reward or punish American Indians based on their incorporation into clearly recognized political entities.

Scholder's work is commercially successful. In the context of the cumulative one-man show at the Smithsonian, he is described as "the most influential, prolific, and controversial figure in the history of native art."[23] His statements on identity are clear, such as in this excerpt from a 1981 interview: "I know almost every prominent Indian in this country and there is one great difference between me and them. Their whole life is lived in a dichotomy, a tug between their tradition and having to live in a non-Indian dominated society. A lot play it very cool, but let me tell you, they HATE it. I don't have any of those feelings. I didn't grow up Indian."[24] According to the exhibit curator Smith, Scholder's legacy is "a life lived in opposition to the prevailing sentiments that offered easy answers to complicated issues. It would have been so easy for Scholder to declare himself, finally, an Indian, to become Luiseño or Hopi or Sioux, and he never did."[25] Scholder's work evidences a conceptual framework in which explicitly Native American arts (often described by the artist's ethnic bylines or labels) are viewed as "ghettoizing,"[26] "imposing,"[27] or "romanticized."[28] The artistic role advocated by Scholder is one of the culturally isolated individual who is free from societal constraints.

Two Native art shows held concurrent with the Scholder exhibits similarly dealt with Native identity. One, titled *Post-Identity* at the Nicole Fiacco Gallery in Hudson, New York, attacked the "false boundaries of culture, market and law that are irrelevant to (Native Artist's) work and their person. . . . For artists, the difference between 'Native American Artist' and an artist who happens to be Native American . . . can mean the difference between having to recapitulate an imposed 'identity' versus the type of self-actualization that artists are especially entitled to."[29] All artists, in this sense, should exercise not only the rights of the individual, but also the super-organic rights of an artist. The other related exhibit, titled *Remix: New Modernities in a Post-Indian World*, organized by the Heard Museum and the Smithsonian National Museum of the American Indian, similarly epitomized the post-Indian movement. As the Native cocurator Gerald McMaster states, "For many Native artists today, cultural identity is not a concern."[30]

Native artists' assertions of oppression and desired liberation are built on the premise that "serious artists of Native American descent" must either "respond against the notion that 'identity' is singular and

that their artwork must comply with stereotypical and legal definitions of 'Native American Art,'"[31] or refuse to engage the concept of
identity at all. It is this concept of freedom that I wish to interrogate:
Freedom from what? Are we to be freed from our own heritage? A post-
Indian platform may sound liberatory, but this stance actually reifies
the power of a colonial mind-set. It allows the audience to maintain a
narrow interpretative field of cultural belonging in which one's spiritual, familial, and cultural influences are equated with state-imposed
recognition policies. Post-Indian ideologies in an extremist sense easily
connote the effect of assimilation. The luxury of rejecting one's affiliation to a tribal nation in this frame of reference in fact constitutes the
act of self-colonization—something to which Native artists seem particularly susceptible.

Post-identity claims evidence a lack of engagement in the concrete realities of racism. A denial of race, either as a biological or social construct, conveniently and effectively silences the realities under
which most Native American populations live. Native Americans are
among the poorest ethnic groups in the United States (28.4 percent live
in poverty—almost twice the rate for the nation as a whole, 15.3 percent).[32] In addition to being vulnerable to poverty, American Indians
experience higher rates of violence than the rest of the population; the
incidence of aggravated assault is twice the national average. Native
women are particularly at risk in this regard: one out of three American
Indian women are raped during their lifetime. Native women are sexu-
ally assaulted three times more than their counterparts. Seventy percent
of these crimes are committed by someone of a different race, indicating troubling connections between racism, violence, and sexism.[33] We
do not live in a race-blind society, despite the claims post-identity ad-
vocates. In fact, these undeniable divides, gender inequalities, ageism,
homophobia, and disabilities critiques unique to the Native American
social landscape are largely unavailable in such projects that deny or
minimize race.

I agree with post-Indian curators that conventional exhibit methodologies restrict accurate and sensitive interpretations of Native
Americans. Specifically, the exhibition of human beings as sideshow
objects, which often occurred in early world's fairs or even in the form
of the collection and curation of human ancestors, still haunts us today.
Perhaps it is this historically situated and contextually specific trauma
that fuels the rejection of identity in contemporary post-Indian exhibition practices. This legacy of representational appropriations and abuse
mirrors the multigenerational trauma of similar government-enacted
policies, such as off-reservation boarding school policies, forced reloca-
tion, and environmental degradation. Public recognition of the horrific
collection, curation, and exhibition of Indian peoples as objects would
do much to sensitize contemporary Native arts audiences to the nega-

tive effects of typecasting, labeling, and classification. Documentation of these practices via film, print, poetry, and exhibitions continue to be important contributions to broadening these discussions.

What exactly does the "artist first, Indian second" perspective signify? I interpret this phrase as indicating a series of rejections. "Artist first" is a rejection of false and biased categorization. The clearest example of this practice I have documented is the Diné artist Mike McCabe, reporting about an instance when he approached a contemporary art gallery in person to inquire if they were taking new artists. McCabe was told, "We don't show Indian art." However when he sent in slides anonymously, the gallery responded enthusiastically, a response that implied that racism was a factor in their decision-making process.[34] Another rejection inherent in the "artist first" claim is that the artist was never Indian, or minimized his or her Indian identity. Fritz Scholder falls neatly into this category. Yet a third rejection of "artist first" is the critique of group Indian art exhibits that appear to present Native arts as the anonymous crafts genre of the past. This argument has merit, yet there are plenty of museums that consistently exhibit solo Indian art shows without rejecting the ethnic association (e.g., the Wheelwright Museum of Santa Fe).

The more difficult task is to ascertain what exactly is being advocated under the rubric "artist first." The lack of interpretative resources available to the average Native arts audience should not be a rationale to reject identity. An engagement with cultural values such as mentorship, reciprocity, and respect, which are often present in other contexts where Native arts circulate, may directly and effectively address this ignorance. Specifically, the conceptual infrastructure of Native arts education in its broadest sense, from language retention and cultural resource management to the establishment of graduate degree programs in Native American art history, can and should be funded and mobilized.

Native arts curatorial practices are hampered not only by the audience's ignorance (a surface interpretation—the effect), but also by a colonial, Western, and patriarchal curation methodology (the cause). Engagement with Native American intellectual traditions—what I term American Indian Curatorial Practice—can champion Native ideologies without falling victim to narrow interpretative strategies of "no word" and "artist first."

AMERICAN INDIAN CURATORIAL PRACTICE

How does one then go about defining an Indigenous framework? In academia there exists a parallel disagreement over how scholars theorize identity politics. Many argue that referencing collective ethnic or social values is an essentialist and outdated theoretical approach.

Theorizing about identity through this anti-identity-politics perspective in fact suggests a false starting point, since all identities are social constructions—fictions that often constrain rather than liberate. This critique of identity politics is closely aligned with current post-identity Native art claims.

Native artists and theorists may be unaware of the rich theoretical debates raging in the academy against identity-based social struggles by those on the left and right. As the post-positivist realism scholars Linda Alcoff and Satya Mohanty state, "For those on the Right, these [identity] movements appear to be threatening individual freedom, while for those on the Left, they are seen as threatening the progressive coalition and wallowing in victimization."[35] The Native arts critique against identity politics draws from both conservative and democratic values, championing individual freedom and seeking cross-cultural alliances.

What is not considered is how minority-based identity curatorial strategies, specifically, American Indian Curatorial Practices, may be better equipped to analyze the complexity of identity constructs than this movement toward the wholesale rejection of identity. Paula Moya proposes a "realist" theory in which "people are neither wholly determined by the social categories through which we are recognized, nor can we ever be free of them."[36] Moya concludes, "seeing identities as things we would be better off without is not the most productive or accurate way to understand them."[37]

The intellectual platform of American Indian Curatorial Practices can assist in understanding the sovereign curatorial strategies employed by many Native curators today who choose to forward collective cultural values. Here I qualify American Indian Curatorial Practice as work that is long-term, mutually meaningful, reciprocal, and with mentorship—all collective constructs. Yet this hopeful analysis must also avoid the divisive polarities of individual versus collective to reach a more nuanced and accurate representation of Indigeneity. As Erica Lord observes, "Considering the history of 'identity art,' I want to explore the next wave of cultural examination, an evolution of new ways to demonstrate cultural identity beyond the polar ideas that exist in a solely black/white diaspora. I want to challenge ideas of cultural purity as well as discuss ideas of attraction, repulsion, exoticism, and gender or feminist notions. Through art and media, the cultural shapers of this generation, it is time for us to self-determine, to control our representation, and to address modernity, the merging of blood, and the myth of an authentic culture."[38]

This "next wave" of expressions is certain to trouble the evident impasses of Native arts scholarship of the past. The exposure of narrowly restrictive strategies of debate—including the rejection of standard fine arts categories of reception ("no word for art in my language") and the assimilation of these same fine arts concepts ("I'm an artist first and an Indian second," or post-Indianness) is critical for the advancement of more accurate terms of engagement. While emerging points of reference that encompass the complex and at times contradictory references of political recognition, social realities, and structural oppressions are emerging, the general public (including the producers and consumers of Native arts) rarely distinguish these developments from the older, more problematic approaches that rely on divisive and simplistic catchphrases. A disconcerting tendency that requires our attention is the likely split between the still ill-conceived popular notions of Nativeness in popular arts circulation (commercial outlets, Indian fairs and markets, etc.) and the more selective (and some may claim elitist) circles of information exchange that push back to interrogate these concepts in the academy and the institution of the museum. This type of class-based divide will surely be cause for concern as the field of Native arts matures.

The primary emerging platform for developing a more accurate portrayal of the field is the institution of the symposium—a narrowly based yet far more productive social networking tool for advancing conversations around Indigeneity and identity in the arts. Significantly, these gatherings are characterized as multi-institutional partnerships that vary from the typical academic proceedings due to their active inclusion of artists, curators, and scholars. In 2009 the School for Advanced Research Indian Arts Research Center in Santa Fe, New Mexico, hosted the seminar "Essential Aesthetics: An Exploration of Contemporary Indigenous Art and Identity," with participation from the Canadian curator Gerald McMaster, the Santa Clara artist Nora Naranjo-Morse, Robert Jahnke of the School of Maori Studies at Massey University in New Zealand, and the Ainu performance artist Mina Sakai, among others. The Diné curator Kathleen Ash-Milby of Smithsonian National Museum of the American Indian served as a co-convener with Mario Caro of the John W. Draper Interdisciplinary Program in Humanities and Social Thought at New York University.

The "Essential Aesthetics" seminar description provided an impetus for discussion of "current individual and communal formulations of Native identity":

> Since the early 1990s, art production that addresses issues of racial, ethnic, sexual, and class identity have been placed under the rubric of "identity politics." More recently, however, there have been attempts by artists, curators, and arts institutions to move beyond these concerns by avoiding groupings along these categories. . . .

. . . How can claims of post-Indianness be considered from community perspectives that may have an essentialist understanding of identity? In other words, is the easy dismissal of a Native identity—an anti-essentialist move that relies on a formulation of identity as constructed—possible for members whose communities believe in identity as inherent?[39]

These timely conversations enacted in the smaller setting of an invited seminar were ultimately expanded by the two organizers, Caro and Ash-Milby, as a public symposium with an open call for papers. Titled "Essentially Indigenous? Contemporary Native Arts Symposium," the conference was held in early May 2011 in New York City at the Diker Pavilion of the George Gustav Heye Center at the National Museum of the American Indian (NMAI). The symposium narrative read, "In the past, many discussions about Native art have focused mostly on the identity of the artist. While Indian identity has a place in the ongoing dialogue about Native art, our intention for this symposium is to break new ground by focusing on the art. What is it about a work of art by a Native artist that makes it Native? Iconography, subject matter, or aesthetic sensibility? Is it a relationship to land or ties to traditional art forms? Is there something essential we can or should define?"[40]

This larger convening of over a hundred people was made possible by sponsorship provided by the NMAI, the Ford Foundation, the Native Peoples Forum (an organization founded at New York University), and the School for Advanced Research. These institutional supports are important to note because while they indicate a certain interiority to these debates, the location of dialogue and discussion in settings that had only a decade or two been seen as alien or even hostile in their reception of calls to Indigeneity are currently enabling progressive debate.[41] The ultimate and broader implications for these types of collaborations must be further assessed for their impact and importance in establishing centers of advancement for intellectual and political Native causes.

While it is too early yet to assess the outcomes of these convenings, it is significant to observe both the broad participation in conversation by emerging and established scholars, writers, and artists and the general tenor of the dialogues engaged in. For example, David Garneau of the University of Regina presented "Necessary Essentialism and Contemporary Aboriginal Art," in which he argues, "Materialist critiques of essentialism are based on a disbelief in metaphysics (Derrida) and meta-narratives (Lyotard). This is in conflict with Aboriginal worldviews and historical experience which usually includes metaphysical beliefs, an essential belonging to place and a history of being caught up in multiple master-narratives. It is time to rethink the essentialism/ materialist binary in order to construct new critical tools that combine contemporary critical thinking and Indigenous epistemology in order to understand contemporary Aboriginal art and its future possibilities."[42] A proactive stance, engagement with established theoretical modes of interrogation and an assertion of the uniqueness of an Indigenous appraisal from within the setting of theory building, is a noteworthy qualification that distinguishes these conversations from earlier, "he said, she said" types of conversations, which lacked the substantial intervention into both the sites and the ideologies of what might loosely be termed more mainstream settings.

Similarly, the artist, academic, and activist Dylan A. T. Miner states, "I directly confront *hybridity* as an empty signifier and hegemonic colonial category, one artists and critics must write against," arguing instead for an Indigenous perspective: "Although post-colonial thinkers have attempted to liberate hybridity from its racialist origins and relationship to botanical crossbreeding, I remain unconvinced about hybridity's efficacy for Indigenous intellectual labor."[43] These examples make plain to me that there is an active engagement in existing premises, and an equally active assertion of alternative ideologies. This intellectual rigor to my mind is evidence of a sea change from previous outright rejections of existing categories to a construction and articulation of counter-narratives, drawn from thought traditions that originate in pre-contact settings. This form of owning and naming parallels other developments in museum theory and holds exciting potential as a bridge for the establishment and codification of Indigenous aesthetic norms.

What makes American Indian Curatorial Practices unique? Why are these approaches that insist on an accounting of history, exposure of injustice, and recognition of cultural values better suited to an analysis of Indigenous arts than the incorporation of Western discursive practices of form, content, and meaning? These questions must be clearly defined, and the answers honestly sought if the new paradigms are to serve as more than reworked forms of older arguments. It is clear now that the dynamism and vibrancy of American Indian arts cannot be expressed in the fine arts vocabulary currently available. In fact, the field of current Native art production exceeds our capacity to engage its intellectual parameters productively. Identifying and critiquing patterns of previous discourse is a prerequisite to the development of any intellectual inquiry. Contemporary American Indian arts, as a central component of American Indian arts scholarship, has the potential to substantially inform our understanding of the contemporary lived realities of Native peoples and communities, reflecting our complexity and resilience.

Nancy Marie Mithlo is a Chiricahua Apache, a PhD, and associate professor of art history and American Indian studies at the University of Wisconsin, Madison. She is the author of *"Our Indian Princess": Subverting the Stereotype* (2009). Mithlo's extensive relationship with the Institute of American Indian Arts includes serving as senior editor for the Ford Foundation–funded volume *Manifestations: New Native Art Criticism*, produced and published by the Museum of Contemporary Native Arts. She received the 2011–2012 School for Advanced Research Anne Ray Fellowship and a Georgia O'Keeffe Research Center Fellowship in support of her publication and exhibit on the legacy of Kiowa photographer Horace Poolaw. Mithlo's curatorial work has resulted in six exhibits at the Venice Biennale.

NOTES

1 Nancy J. Parezo, "The Challenge of Native American Art and Material Culture," *Museum Anthropology* 14, no. 4 (1990): 12–29.

2 Margaret Archuleta and Rennard Strickland, *Shared Visions: Native American Painters and Sculptors of the Twentieth Century* (Phoenix: Heard Museum, 1991), 8.

3 The lack of resources for American Indian arts (and especially contemporary American Indian arts) was addressed by the Ford Foundation's 2010 report "Native Arts and Cultures: Research, Growth, and Opportunities for Philanthropic Support," http://www.fordfoundation.org/pdfs/library/Native-Arts-and-Cultures.pdf. See also Nancy Marie Mithlo, "Visiting," published in 2008 an outgrowth of the Ford-funded "American Indian Curatorial Practice: State of the Field" conference, available at http://www.nancymariemithlo.com/aicp_menu.htm.

4 Arjun Appadurai, *The Social Life of Things: Commodities in Cultural Perspective* (Cambridge: Cambridge University Press, 1986).

5 Jamake Highwater, *The Primal Mind: Vision and Reality in Indian America* (New York: Harper and Row, 1981), 55, 69–70.

6 Kathryn Shanley, "The Indians America Loves to Love and Read: American Indian Identity and Cultural Appropriation," in *Native American Representations: First Encounters, Distorted Images, and Literary Appropriations*, ed. Gretchen M. Bataille (Lincoln: University of Nebraska Press, 2001), 26–51.

7 Gussie Fauntleroy, "No Word for Art—Only Meaning," *Pasatiempo, Santa Fe New Mexican*, October 9–15, 1992, 7.

8 Leatrice Mikkelsen, *Decolonizing the Mind: End of a 500-Year Era* (Seattle: Center on Contemporary Art, 1992).

9 Janet Catherine Berlo and Ruth B. Phillips, *Native North American Art* (New York: Oxford University Press, 1998), 9.

10 Julia Harrison, "Ideas of Museum in the 1990s," in *Heritage, Museums, and Galleries: An Introductory Reader*, ed. Gerard Corsane (New York: Routledge, 2005), 40.

11 Ibid., 43.

12 Edward Halealoha Ayau, "Bishop Museum Doesn't Qualify as a

Claimant to Artifacts," *Honolulu Star-Bulletin*, August 29, 2004.

13 Documentation of a Native American artist feigning naïveté to increase sales is difficult to come by, but this is a topic that deserves further inquiry. The sale of high-end Indian arts in key regional locations during the 1980s also remains largely undocumented. For a pertinent case study involving a prominent dealer, see Jori Finkel, "Is Everything Sacred? A Respected Art Dealer Is Busted for Selling a Cheyenne War Bonnet," *Legal Affairs*, July/August 2003.

14 Erica Lord, online audio interview, Native American Indigenous Cinema and Art, 2006, http://thenaica.org/edition_three/index.html.

15 James Clifford, *The Predicament of Culture* (Cambridge: Harvard University Press, 2002).

16 Tom Hill, "A Question of Survival" in *All Roads Are Good: Native Voices on Life and Culture*, ed. Terrance Winch (Washington: Smithsonian Institution Press, 1994), 191.

17 Sally Price, *Primitive Art in Civilized Places* (Chicago: University of Chicago Press, 1989), 89.

18 Christian F. Feest, *Native Arts of North America* (London: Thames and Hudson, 1980), 9, 14.

19 Berlo and Phillips, *Native North American Art*, 9.

20 Ward Churchill, "American Indian Art and Artists: In Search of a Definition," Newsletter of the Leonard Peltier Defense Committee, November/December 1992.

21 The exhibit *Remix: New Modernities in a Post-Indian World*, organized by the Heard Museum and the Smithsonian National Museum of the American Indian (curated by Gerald McMaster and Joe Baker), epitomized the post-Indian movement. The George Gustav Heye Center of the National Museum of the American Indian in New York hosted the exhibit from June 7 to September 21, 2008. See http://www.nmai.si.edu/exhibitions/remix. A negative review by the *Globe and Mail* art critic Sarah Milroy prompted a discussion McMaster, Baker, Milroy, and the professor of African and African Diaspora art history and visual culture Salah Hassan at the Art Gallery of Ontario, on August 23, 2009. An audio recording of the event is available at http://www.ago.net/are-we-past-the-age-of-an-aboriginal-art-show.

22 Smithsonian National Museum of the American Indian, "Indian/Not Indian," nd, http://www.nmai.si.edu/exhibitions/scholder/introduction.html.

23 Ibid.

24 Paul Chaat Smith, "Monster Love," in *Fritz Scholder: Indian/Not Indian*, ed. Lowery Stokes Sims, Truman T. Lowe, and Paul Chaat Smith (New York: Prestel, 2008), 33. Original quote from Ed Montini, "Four Sides of Fritz," *Arizona Republic*, February 22, 1981.

25 Ibid., 35.

26 Richard Nilsen, "Artist First, Indian Second: Native Artists Embrace Multicultural World," *Arizona Republic*, September 27, 2007.

27 Nicole Fiacco Gallery, Hudson, New York, *Post-Identity* exhibition press, 2007. Unfortunately, the gallery and its Web site are not active at the time of this printing in 2011.

28 Eleanor Heartney, "Native Art in an Age of Hybridity," in *Remix: New Modernities in a Post-Indian World*, ed. Joe Baker and Gerald McMaster

(Washington: National Museum of the American Indian, 2008), 37.

29 Fiacco Gallery.

30 Gerald McMaster, "Introductions: Mixing It Up," in Baker and McMaster, *Remix*, 57.

31 Fiacco Gallery.

32 U.S. Census Bureau, 2010 American Community Survey, nd, available at http://factfinder2.census.gov/.

33 Amnesty International, "United States of America: Maze of Injustice: The Failure to Protect Indigenous Women from Violence in the USA," April 24, 2007, http://www.amnestyusa.org/pdfs/MazeOfInjustic.pdf.

34 Nancy Marie Mitchell (Mithlo), "The Negotiated Role of Contemporary American Indian Artists: A Study in Marginality" (Stanford University, 1993).

35 Linda Martin Alcoff and Satya P. Mohanty, "Reconsidering Identity Politics: An Introduction," in *Identity Politics Reconsidered*, ed. Linda Martin Alcoff, Michael Hames-Garcia, Satya P. Mohanty, and Paula M. L. Moya (New York: Palgrave Macmillan, 2006), 2.

36 Paula Moya, "What's Identity Got to Do with It? Mobilizing Identities in the Multicultural Classroom," in Alcoff et al., *Identity Politics Reconsidered*, 99.

37 Ibid., 101.

38 Lord, Native American Indigenous Cinema and Art.

39 "Essential Aesthetics: An Exploration of Contemporary Indigenous Art and Identity," November 16–20, 2009, http://sarweb.org/index.php?iarc_contemporary_native_arts.

40 "Essentially Indigenous? Contemporary Native Arts Symposium," May 5–6, 2011, http://www.nmai.si.edu/subpage.cfm?subpage=collaboration&second=seminars#.

41 It is significant to note also the focus on the art object in the call for participation at the symposium's museum location, rather than the more theory-based, contextual seminar setting of School for Advanced Research.

42 David Garneau abstract, "Necessary Essentialism and Contemporary Aboriginal Art," provided by the conference organizers of "Essentially Indigenous? Contemporary Native Arts Symposium," May 5–6, 2011, George Gustav Heye Center, National Museum of the American Indian, New York.

43 Dylan A. T. Miner, "An Indigenist Provocation on/as Contemporary Art: A Migration Story in Seven Fragments," provided by the conference organizers of "Essentially Indigenous? Contemporary Native Arts Symposium," May 5–6, 2011, George Gustav Heye Center, National Museum of the American Indian, New York.

The Death of Raymond Yellow Thunder, and Other True Stories from the Nebraska–Pine Ridge Border Towns

by Stew Magnuson
Texas Tech University Press, 2011

The Death of Raymond Yellow Thunder tells the story of the brutal 1972 killing of a Lakota man, Raymond Yellow Thunder, in Gordon, Nebraska. Yellow Thunder died from injuries sustained during a beating by several white perpetrators. Yellow Thunder's death is often credited as igniting an onslaught of American Indian activism in the 1970s, and as one of the main events that brought the American Indian Movement to media fame and to the forefront of American Indian activism. Stew Magnuson's book additionally focuses on the death of Yellow Thunder in relation to other racial incidents in the Nebraska–Pine Ridge reservation border towns of Gordon and Whiteclay. The stories of the people, both white and Indian, who populate these border towns are interwoven throughout the text. Magnuson characterizes these border areas as dark, complex, and dismal small towns that are plagued with alcohol abuse and narrow-minded bigotry.

American Indian people historically have a contentious history with the non-Indian towns that border their nations. These towns, commonly referred to as border towns, are fraught with long-standing racial tensions and prejudices. Magnuson argues that the prejudices in the Nebraska context are two-sided, with the American Indians portrayed not as helpless victims of crime but often as participants in the racial dynamics played out in the border towns (301, 303). Unfortunately, the events described in *The Death of Raymond Yellow Thunder* are not uncommon stories in Indian Country. Nor are these incidents relegated solely to the past.

Most recently, on May 24, 2011, an American Indian family in Nevada was the target of a skinhead attack. The family was harassed at a gas station by a group of skinheads and then pursued down a highway. An American Indian man, his son, and his wife were beaten severely. The perpetrators in this gruesome attack have not been arrested, and one of them is the son of the local sheriff.[1] During April 2010, in Farmington, New Mexico, two white men and one mixed-blood Navajo man branded a young mentally disabled Navajo man with swastikas. Two of the perpetrators in this attack have been sentenced and charged with hate crimes.[2] Even though hate crimes committed against American Indians are common, they are not often discussed in the media or literature. It is important to expose these issues because they are a reality for many American Indian people and a violation of their human and civil rights.

This book was originally was published in 2008. The paperback version has been revised and updated, and includes a new afterword. The prologue begins with a march in Whiteclay, Nebraska, on July 3, 1999, after an American Indian man was found beaten to death there. As in the past, family members called in the American Indian Movement to help coordinate a march and protest against racial violence and mistreatment of American Indians in Whiteclay. Magnuson, a journalist, covers these events along with the 1999 march. The vivid description of the march and protest provides an introduction to the subsequent chapters, which depict both the death of Raymond Yellow Thunder and the history of racial tension in this region that dates back to the first contact between soldiers and Indians.

The chapter "A Cold Night in Gordon" relays the terrible events surrounding the beating of Yellow Thunder on February 12, 1972, and his subsequent death. Brothers Les and Pat Hare, along with Robert Bayliss, Bernard Lutter, and Jeanette Thompson, were drinking and joyriding in the small town of Gordon when they came upon Yellow Thunder walking along the road. In some reservation border towns, beating up Indians is a common pastime for white youths. Yellow Thunder was offered a ride, then was stripped of his pants and thrown into an American Legion hall. His attackers hunted him down for a second round of attacks later the same night. Yellow Thunder died several days later from brain hemorrhaging. Magnuson fleshes out the story and describes the night like a scene from a novel, and explains the personalities of the attackers and their possible motivations. According to Magnuson, he drew from interviews, newspaper articles, court records, and interviews with relatives of Yellow Thunder. At times, however, it is unclear from where he derives his information.

Magnuson inserts history to provide the reader with the context for the death of Raymond Yellow Thunder. In historical chapters like "The Story of John Gordon," Magnuson explains that gold prospectors and squatters founded Gordon, Nebraska, along with other towns in Lakota country. John Gordon was prospecting for gold, and the town of Gordon was settled by missionaries and named after him. The history of this region is vicious, and the squatters and prospectors were violating the treaty of 1868, encroaching on Lakota lands. For these historical sections of the book, Magnuson relies heavily on history as told from the white historian perspective. This is where oral histories and interviews from American Indian people would have provided a more evenhanded version of history. The book goes back and forth between the events from the 1970s, the nineteenth century, and the present day. Three consecutive chapters explain the history of the white border town residents and prominent Indian figures. Magnuson focuses on the Indian wars in this region, with sections on Red Cloud, the theft of the Black Hills, the Fetterman Massacre, and the Massacre at Wounded Knee. This history is helpful in terms of understanding the race relations in the 1970s and in the present day, as it provides a backdrop for Yellow Thunder's murder investigation and the trial of the accused.

Most compelling in Magnuson's narrative are the perspectives and stories about American Indian Movement leaders such as Bob Yellow Bird and the family members of Raymond Yellow Thunder. Interviews with Yellow Thunder's niece take the reader through the family's heartbreaking discovery of her uncle's death and the family's pursuit for justice. The Hare brothers were deemed most responsible for Yellow Thunder's death because they were the primary assailants. They were charged with manslaughter and false imprisonment and sentenced to ten years in prison, but they did not serve their full sentences. The other perpetrators were charged with false imprisonment.

The book is a narrative and reads like a piece of fiction, with main characters and a developed story. It is a bit reminiscent of Rodney Barker's *The Broken Circle* (1992), about the brutal killing of a Navajo man by white teenagers, which was also written in a narrative style. However, Magnuson's narrative at times takes away from first-person accounts of the participants and replaces their voice with that of the author's. The narrative is questionable when the author uses an omniscient voice. While describing the beating of Raymond Yellow Thunder, Magnuson describes Yellow Thunder's inner dialogue, such as when he writes, "It was the shame he felt most" (24). Magnuson continues to presume that Yellow Thunder was too ashamed to spend the night at his niece's house, which is why Magnuson argues that Yellow Thunder wandered the streets of Gordon the night of his murder. Magnuson makes too many assumptions and draws too many conclusions about the events of that night. The reader is left to wonder how Magnuson knew what people in history felt or thought, especially those who are no longer living. In the notes section, Magnuson lists numerous interviews; however, the way the narrative and the notes are written makes it difficult to discern between interviews and the author's recollection.

Magnuson's journalism background would have been better served had he left in the text the voices of the people he interviewed. The strongest statement in the book comes from the only direct quote. Dennis Yellow Thunder, Raymond Yellow Thunder's nephew, explains that he is not hateful and that in Lakota tradition, "We pray for our enemy so that they do not do it again" (320).

Magnuson is an engaging storyteller and *The Death of Raymond Yellow Thunder* is an easy narrative to read for those unfamiliar with the topic of border town racial violence. But it is primarily written for a non-Indian audience, and not at all for an academic audience. An American Indian perspective on this topic is definitely needed. Magnuson covered the events in 1999 as a journalist, but he offers little analysis. The author provides no answers, instead noting that "not a damn thing would change" (291, 294, 299, 305) regarding the racism in the region. The reader is left with the idea that the racial atmosphere in Pine Ridge border towns will not improve, and Magnuson asserts that the prejudices are a result of "people who want to believe the worst of each other" (303).

AUTHOR BIOGRAPHY

Cheryl Redhorse Bennett is Diné from the Navajo Nation in Shiprock, New Mexico. She is of the Naneessht'ezhi clan and descended from the Comanche people on her father's side. She is a PhD candidate at the University of Arizona, majoring in American Indian studies. Her research interests include hate crimes committed against Navajos and American Indians, contemporary American Indian governments, and violence against American Indian women.

NOTES

1 See http://indiancountrytoday
medianetwork.com/2011/07/
waiting-for-justice-living-in-fear/.

2 See http://64.38.12.138/
News/2011/002729.asp.

REVIEW ESSAY *by Rebecca Tsosie*

In the Courts of the Conqueror: The 10 Worst Indian Law Cases Ever Decided

by Walter R. Echo-Hawk
Fulcrum Press, 2010

The eminent American jurist Learned Hand once said, "The spirit of liberty is the spirit which is not too sure that it is right."[1] Walter Echo-Hawk's foray into the "ten worst Indian law cases ever decided" offers a stunning testimony in support of that observation. Unlike other fields of American jurisprudence, such as property law, torts, or criminal law, federal Indian law derives not from British common law, but from the political interactions of separate sovereigns, the Native nations of these lands and the British Crown, and its successor, the United States of America. Although these sovereign interactions once assumed the currency of international relations, through negotiated treaties, the United States took an unprecedented level of control over what became "domestic dependent nations," and engaged in a subsequent attack on the political sovereignty of Native nations. This has culminated in a set of current conditions that significantly depart from the standards of justice articulated in the U.S. Constitution, such as liberty and equality, or in international conventions detailing the political right of self-determination that belongs to all "peoples."

Despite these realities, most citizens of the United States continue to believe that Native Americans now enjoy "equal citizenship" within U.S. democratic society, and they often wonder why Native peoples get "special rights," such as the ability to engage in casino gaming on the reservation. As Echo-Hawk points out, part of this belief can be attributed to the fact that there is a "serious information gap about Native Americans in the United States," because most Americans "have never met or talked to an Indian, have never been on an Indian reservation, and know very little about Native Americans in general" (13). Native history and culture are not part of the standard curriculum taught within public schools, and even within American universities a student would have to make a special effort to secure this knowledge through American Indian studies classes, where these are available, or through other courses where the faculty possess the knowledge to teach the subject effectively.

Echo-Hawk's book makes a notable contribution to the literature on federal Indian law, as well as American Indian history and policy. Walter Echo-Hawk, a member of the Pawnee Nation, is renowned within the field of Indian law as one of the foremost litigators for Native American rights in the country. He served as a staff attorney at the Native American Rights Fund for over thirty-five years, charting legal recognition for tribal rights to land, water, and cultural resources, as well as protecting the rights of individual Native Americans to access and protect their religious and cultural liberties. Echo-Hawk's steadfast advocacy resulted in many victories for Native nations and for Native American prisoners and cultural practitioners, but he also experienced a pervasive frustration with the inability of courts to probe the seamy underbelly of American law and engage the "nefarious legal doctrines" developed by past courts to justify the dispossession and subordination of Native nations. This book results from Echo-Hawk's long-standing experience as a litigator and advocate of Native rights, and it serves two pivotal purposes. First, it provides an accessible and fascinating account of several Supreme Court cases that defined the "rights" of Native peoples and were used as precedent by subsequent federal and state courts. And second, it provides a compelling account of how American law has only rarely served as a "shield to protect Native Americans from abuse and further their aspirations as indigenous peoples," and how its predominant use has been as a "sword to harm Native peoples by stripping away their human rights" (4). Through these inquiries, Echo-Hawk succeeds in developing a framework to evaluate the "justice" effectuated by federal Indian law. The book effectively presents the actual data on what the law is and where it came from, and proves the true impact of federal Indian law as a tool of domination, rather than liberation.

The cases that Echo-Hawk selects are notable because they draw both from the foundational decisions of federal Indian law, and from lesser-known cases that build out the implications of the doctrines. For example, most students of federal Indian law and American Indian studies will read *Johnson v. McIntosh*, the 1823 Supreme Court decision which held that the European nations perfected their title to Native lands by "discovery" and settlement of those lands, while Indian nations retained only the right to "occupancy," pending the ultimate extinguishment of that right by "purchase or conquest." They will also study other pivotal cases, such as *Cherokee Nation v. Georgia* (1831), which held that the Cherokee Nation lacked standing in the U.S. Supreme Court to contest the state of Georgia's blatant effort to abrogate their federally protected treaty rights; and *Lone Wolf v. Hitchcock* (1903), which held that the United States possesses the political right to unilaterally abrogate an Indian treaty and confiscate the Indian nation's lands in its role as a "trustee," and that Native nations could not challenge this action in the U.S. courts because of the "political question doctrine." Such cases explain the devastating loss of land and denial of tribal rights that accompanied westward expansion in the nineteenth century. Echo-Hawk provides a fascinating synthesis of the history that led up to these decisions and their analytical underpinnings. He also demonstrates how these doctrines continued into the twentieth century, in cases such as *Tee-Hit-Ton Indians v. United States*, the 1955 case that applied the fiction of "discovery and conquest" to lands held by Native Alaskan nations, despite the fact that those nations had an entirely different history and context, stemming from their minimal relations with Russia.

However, many students will never encounter the lesser-known cases that Echo-Hawk features in this book. For example, *Connors v. United States and Cheyenne Indians* is an 1898 case filed in the U.S. Court of Claims by a Nebraska rancher seeking to recover damages under the Indian Depredation Act of 1891 for the alleged loss of livestock occasioned by a group of Cheyenne Indians. The holding in that case is unexceptional. The rancher's claim was denied on the basis that the Indians were, at the time of the event, "at war" with the United States, rather than "at peace," which was a statutory ground for recovery. Through the extensive background history that Echo-Hawk develops, however, the reader gains an invaluable glimpse into the realities of the day, including the aftermath of the 1864 Sand Creek Massacre, in which 160 Cheyenne and Arapaho Indians were murdered by Colonel John M. Chivington and his militia, their bodies mutilated and displayed during an infamous public parade through Denver, and their skulls subsequently sent back East to be housed within the Smithsonian Museum. Echo-Hawk's discussion of the opinion of a largely unknown nineteenth-century claims court judge reveals the court's uneasy effort to determine the "legal status" of an Indian nation under attack, including the Cheyenne Nation's initial attempts to articulate a relationship of peace with the United States; then its desperate attempt to survive the murderous onslaught of American settlers; and finally the incarceration of tribal members as "prisoners of war" by the U.S. military. Echo-Hawk carefully presents the underlying issue, which is whether the use of force by the United States against Native nations during the Indian Wars could be justified under any existing legal or moral principle. If not, the ensuing killings constituted acts of "murder" and not "war."

In other chapters, Echo-Hawk explores state court opinions that drew on the doctrines of U.S. Supreme Court cases, as well as the pervasive social attitudes favoring the cultural assimilation of Native people and denying their cultural and religious liberties. For example, *In re Adoption of John Doe v. Heim* is a 1976 New Mexico appellate court decision that illustrates the widespread pattern of state courts to confiscate Indian children from their families during child dependency proceedings and place them for adoption by non-Indian families on the grounds that this was in the "best interest" of the Indian child. Echo-Hawk offers an account of the courageous (and unsuccessful) effort of a Navajo child's extended family to keep the child, and then details the response of the state agency and court, which effectively dismissed the cultural claims of the family, as well as the political interest of the Navajo nation to decide the adoption of any member within its own tribal court. Echo-Hawk shows how similar cases nationwide set the tone for the Indian Child Welfare Act, which was passed by Congress in 1978 to validate the cultural and political rights of Native nations to retain control over adoptions involving tribal members.

Similarly, Echo-Hawk discusses the 1982 decision of a California Court of Appeals in *Wana the Bear v. Community Construction*, which held that a Miwok burial ground was not subject to legal protection under the California cemetery law because it had not been "used continuously as a graveyard without interruption for five years" pursuant to the state statute. The court's cramped reading of the statute paved the way for the development of the burial ground and negated the public policy of protecting "places where the dead are buried," as well as the strict letter of the law, which defined a cemetery as a place where "six or more human bodies are buried in one place." Echo-Hawk's discussion of the case reveals the local context of the action, including the genocidal conduct of the state of California toward Native peoples during the gold rush years. He also develops the history of human rights abuses perpetuated by American policy makers, who affirmatively supported the desecration of Native American bodies and burial sites, and the

curation of deceased Native Americans in museum collections throughout the country. This brutal history, which has been documented by
scholars such as James Riding In, ultimately led to the enactment of the
National Museum of the American Indian Act in 1989 and the Native
American Graves Protection and Repatriation Act in 1990.[2] These stat-
utes established the basis for repatriation of Native American human
remains and cultural objects to the affiliated Native nations, as well as
dictating standards to govern future excavations on federal and tribal
lands and laws prohibiting the commercial sale of such items.

Of course, as Echo-Hawk demonstrates in subsequent chapters,
Native American litigants face continued challenges in articulating
their rights to practice their traditional religions and protect their cultures, and they are not able to litigate their constitutional right to religious freedom as "equal citizens." Echo-Hawk offers a comprehensive
and illuminating discussion of the Supreme Court's opinions in *Lyng v.
Northwest Indian Cemetery Association* (1988), which upheld the federal government's right to build a road through a Native American sacred site,
even though this would foreclose their traditional religious practice,
and *Employment Division v. Smith* (1990), which upheld "neutral" criminal
prohibitions against peyote, despite the fact that this would foreclose
members of the Native American Church from practicing their religion.
Echo-Hawk was one of the lead attorneys arguing for the rights of the
Native American Church practitioners in *Smith*, as well as an influential advocate for federal legislation to protect Native American religious
rights. Echo-Hawk offers a compelling account of the history leading up
to the *Smith* case, as well as the congressional attempt to protect the right
of Native practitioners to use the sacrament of peyote through its 1994
amendments to the American Indian Religious Freedom Act.

Of course, the battle to protect Native American sacred sites continues, even though Congress passed the Religious Freedom Restoration
Act (RFRA) and amended that statute to protect some forms of property held by church organizations. The lower federal courts differ as
to whether RFRA's standard for protection of Native American sacred
sites mirrors the constitutional free exercise analysis detailed in *Lyng*,
which subordinates Native religions to the will of the federal agency
as owner and manager of federal public lands, or whether Congress
has established a higher threshold through RFRA, equivalent to the
protections extended to "church property" held by other religious
groups.[3] The U.S. Supreme Court will at some point resolve the issue,
and Echo-Hawk offers a commendable analysis of the issues the Court
will be asked to evaluate.

Walter Echo-Hawk's comprehensive analysis of federal Indian
law succeeds in demonstrating that the "ten worst cases" in Indian law
have little to do with "justice," and are instead based on a potentially
deadly combination of racial stereotyping and colonial doctrine mas-

querading as "law" (5). In that sense, Echo-Hawk asserts, the American legal system does not align with its stated commitment to "equal justice" for all because it continues to perpetuate a form of racism. Echo-Hawk encourages us to seriously engage how we are to "root out these vestiges of racism and colonialism in the law and replace them with legal principles more in keeping with the postcolonial world" (5). Echo-Hawk frames the challenge of achieving justice in a "settler state," such as the United States, given the central mission of building a new empire founded on the "conquest and dispossession of Native peoples" (23). He identifies several of the "far-fetched legal fictions used to decide legal questions in the United States and other settler states," built on notions of the essential superiority of civilized European nations and their duty to Christianize and civilize "savage" peoples in the newly "discovered" lands (44–48). He builds powerful support for these observations in a sustained analysis of the cases, and he courageously defends the argument, made by many scholars, that federal Indian law and policy perpetrated "genocide" and "ethnocide" against Native Americans (399–420).

In the concluding chapter, Echo-Hawk asserts that the Supreme Court should be the "first line of defense" in the effort to reform this dismal history, particularly in view of its historic role in developing the legal justification for genocide and ethnocide. He then advances a clear and articulate charter for legal reform. Echo-Hawk agrees with Judge Learned Hand that the law is a living institution that evolves over time, and that we must always be cognizant of the shortfalls of American law and be committed to effective redress for violations of our fundamental notions of liberty and justice. The lives of Native people in the United States are heavily controlled by American law, in ways that other groups have never experienced. Thus the venerable commitment to adhering to "precedent," which serves the interests of justice in other areas of the law, often perpetuates the fundamental "injustice" that exists at the roots of federal Indian law.

Echo-Hawk makes an effective case for measuring federal Indian law by the standards advocated by the United Nations Declaration on the Rights of Indigenous Peoples, which the UN General Assembly adopted in 2007. Rather than masking federal colonial power with the standard doctrines of federal "plenary power" and the "trust responsibility," Echo-Hawk offers clear proposals to transition the colonial underpinnings of these doctrines into the implementation of Indigenous self-determination by a federal government that protects Native rights along that road. Echo-Hawk draws on the civil rights–era jurisprudence that eventually overcame American apartheid, and argues that a similar transformation might accompany the effort to implement the right of self-determination for Native peoples. Through this vision, the political and cultural sovereignty of Native peoples can be realized within American law and the "dark side" of American federal Indian law will dissolve, setting the stage for a new day, literally and figuratively, in the lives of the Native nations that belong to this land.

AUTHOR BIOGRAPHY

Rebecca Tsosie is professor of law and Willard H. Pedrick Distinguished Research Scholar at the Sandra Day O'Connor College of Law at Arizona State University. She is also a faculty member in the School of Historical, Philosophical, and Religious Studies, and serves as an affiliate professor for the American Indian Studies Program and the School of Sustainability at ASU.

NOTES

1 Gerald Gunther, *Learned Hand: The Man and the Judge* (New York: Alfred A. Knopf, 1994), xiii.

2 See generally James Riding In, "Without Ethics and Morality: A Historical Overview of Imperial Archaeology and American Indians," *Arizona State Law Journal* 24 (Spring 1992): 11–34.

3 See generally *Navajo Nation v. U.S. Forest Service*, 535 F.3d 1058 (9th Cir. 2008), upholding the U.S. Forest Service decision to approve a permit allowing the use of wastewater to create artificial snow for a ski resort on San Francisco Peaks—a sacred site to many Southwest tribes, including the Navajo Nation and Hopi Tribe—on the grounds that RFRA incorporates the same standard as *Lyng*.

FIRST PEOPLES
New Directions in Indigenous Studies

www.firstpeoplesnewdirections.org

UNIVERSITY OF ARIZONA PRESS | UNIVERSITY OF MINNESOTA PRESS
UNIVERSITY OF NORTH CAROLINA PRESS | OREGON STATE UNIVERSITY PRESS

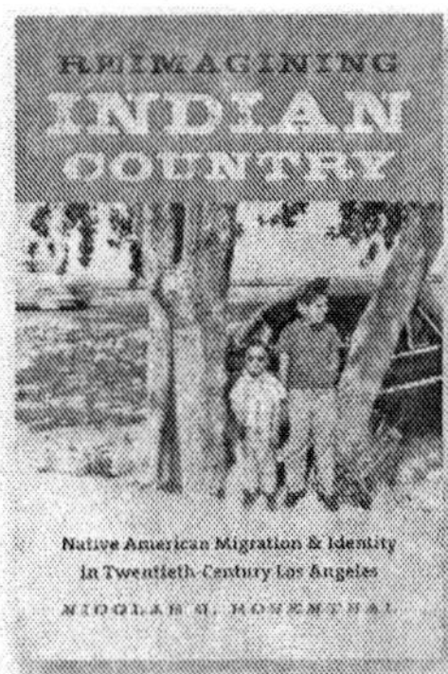

Reimagining Indian Country
*Native American Migration
and Identity in Twentieth-Century Los Angeles*
By Nicholas G. Rosenthal
In the twentieth century, cities have played a defining role in modern American Indian life. Rosenthal emphasizes lived experiences and examines the evolution of Native American identity in recent decades. He argues that Indian identity must be understood as dynamic and fully enmeshed in modern global networks.
Cloth, 6.125 x 9.25, $39.95
UNIVERSITY OF NORTH CAROLINA PRESS
WWW.UNCPRESS.UNC.EDU

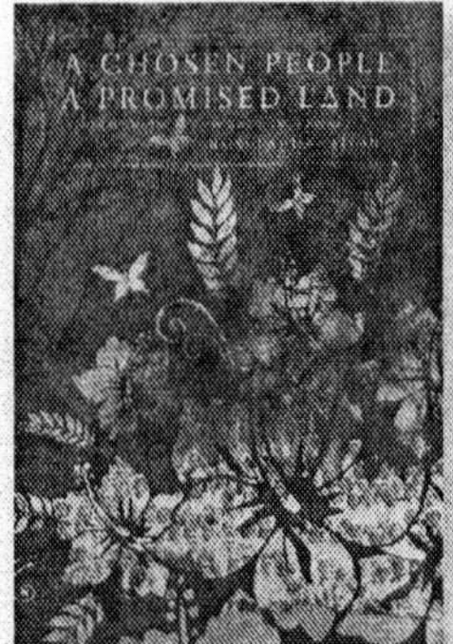

A Chosen People, a Promised Land
Mormonism and Race in Hawai'i
By Hokulani K. Aikau
Using the words of Native Hawaiian Latter-Day Saints to illuminate the intersections of race, colonization, and religion, *A Chosen People, a Promised Land* examines Polynesian Mormon articulations of faith and identity within a larger political context of self-determination.
Paper, 5.5 x 8.5, $22.50
Cloth, 5.5 x 8.5, $67.50
UNIVERSITY OF MINNESOTA PRESS
WWW.UPRESS.UMN.EDU

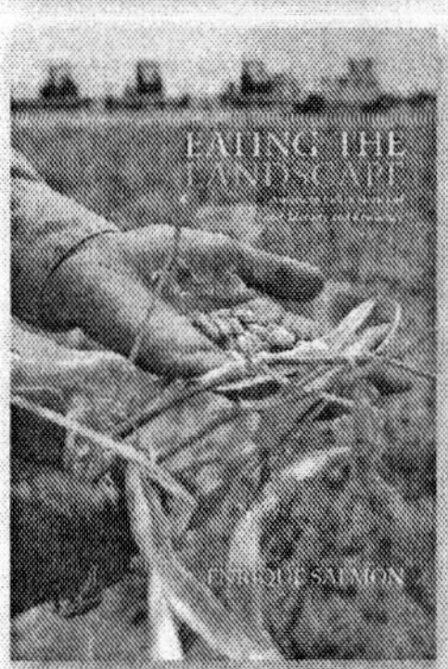

Eating the Landscape
American Indian Stories of Food, Identity, and Resilience
By Enrique Salmón
Renowned Indigenous ethnobotanist Enrique Salmón weaves his historical and cultural knowledge with stories from American Indian farmers to illustrate how Indigenous foodways are deeply rooted in practices or traditions of envirionmental stewardship.
Paper, 6 x 9, $17.95
UNIVERSITY OF ARIZONA PRESS
WWW.UAPRESS.ARIZONA.EDU

Uniting the Tribes
The Rise and Fall of Pan-Indian Community on the Crow Reservation
Frank Rzeczkowski

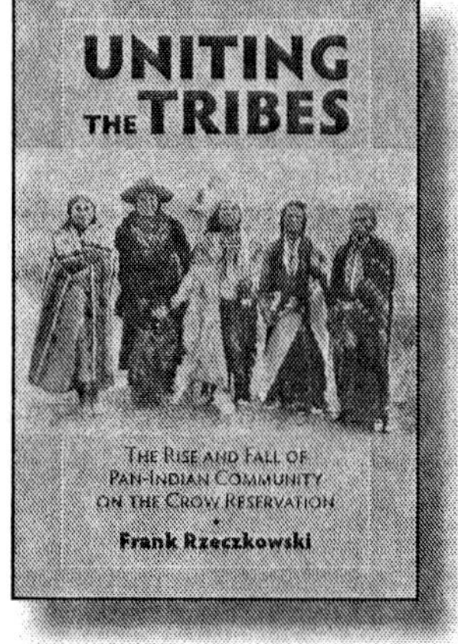

"Rzeczkowski's on-the-ground narrative brilliantly reveals both the rise of cross-tribal identities and the processes that undermined them. His study has much to teach us about Indian peoples and about the uneven power of colonialism."—Fred Hoxie, author of *Parading through History: The Making of the Crow Nation in America, 1805–1935*

"Provides a fresh look at the importance of intertribal relationships and the permeable boundaries of the too often calcified concept of 'tribes.' . . . A welcome addition to the library of Great Plains historians, anthropologists and Native American scholars alike."—Kathleen Sherman, author of *Lakota Culture, World Economy*

336 pages, 18 photographs, Cloth $39.95

Lessons from an Indian Day School
Negotiating Colonization in Northern New Mexico, 1902–1907
Adrea Lawrence

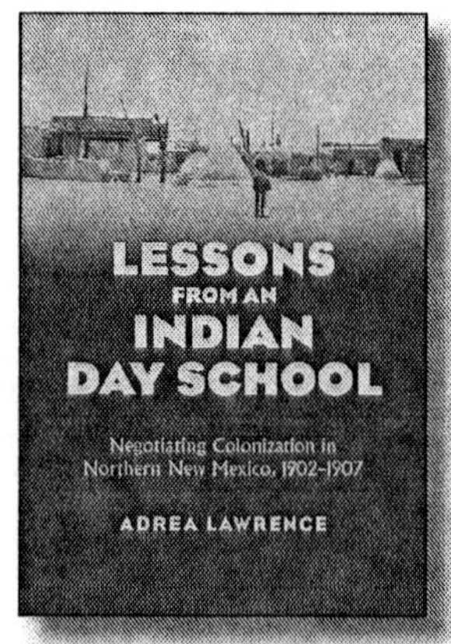

"Lawrence asks us to reassess how and with what consequences Native people encountered both the schools that were designed to destroy their cultures, and the officials who spearheaded the effort. In her hands, this is a complex tale of cross-cultural encounter that reveals a more complicated landscape than we have previously imagined."
—Clyde Ellis, author of *To Change Them Forever: Indian Education at the Rainy Mountain Boarding School, 1893–1920*

312 pages, 17 photographs, 3 maps, Cloth $34.95

 **University Press of Kansas**

Phone 785-864-4155 · Fax 785-864-4586 · www.kansaspress.ku.edu

The Western Historical Quarterly

FOUNDED IN 1969, the *Western Historical Quarterly*, official journal of the Western History Association, presents original articles dealing with the North American West— expansion and colonization, indigenous histories, regional studies (including western Canada, northern Mexico, Alaska, and Hawai'i), and transnational, comparative, and borderland histories. Each issue contains reviews and notices of significant books, as well as recent articles, in the field.

Manuscripts should be submitted in duplicate, text and endnotes doublespaced for a total of no more than 10,000 words. Submissions will be returned only if a stamped, self-addressed envelope is provided. No multiple submissions. Manuscripts, books for review, advertising inquiries, and correspondence should be sent to:

WESTERN HISTORICAL QUARTERLY
Utah State University
0740 Old Main Hill
Logan UT 84322-0740

435.797.1301
whq@usu.edu
www.usu.edu/history/whq

Back issues, article reprints, cumulative article index, and complete microfilm runs are available for purchase.

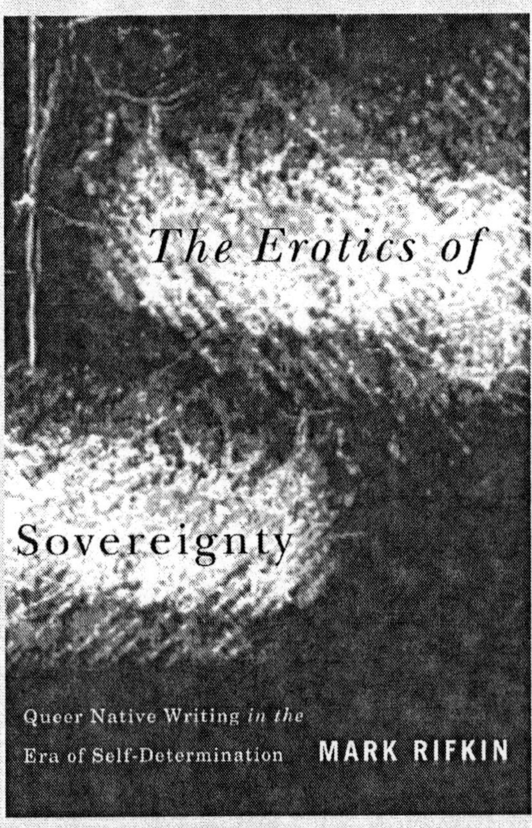

The Erotics of
Sovereignty
Queer Native Writing in the
Era of Self-Determination   MARK RIFKIN